DON'T PICK ON ME

HOW TO HANDLE BULLYING

Rosemary Stones is a psychoanalytic psychotherapist in private practice in Covent Garden, London. She is also the editor of *Books for Keeps*, a children's literature review journal. She wrote this book on bullying because her daughter had been bullied at school and she wished she'd been able to help her more at that time. In her therapy practice now she comes across patients who have experienced bullying so the impact of this behaviour is something that continues to interest her.

DON'T PICK ON ME

HOW TO HANDLE BULLYING

ROSEMARY STONES

Piccadilly Press • London

For Melanie Hart, with love and thanks

First published in Great Britain in 2005
by Piccadilly Press Ltd,
5 Castle Road, London NW1 8PR
www.piccadillypress.co.uk

This edition revised and published in Great Britain in 2011

A catalogue record for this book is available from the British Library

ISBN: 978 1 84812 164 5 (paperback)

1 3 5 7 9 10 8 6 4 2

Print[ed and bound by CPI Group (UK) Ltd, Croydon,] [CR]0 4YY
[...design and typesett]ion by Amanda [H]yn[a]s

Contents

Who Is This Book For?

This book is for people who are being bullied and for people who are bullies.

If you are being bullied I'm sure you would like the bullying to stop, like Chelsea:

Chelsea is convinced that she isn't likeable as no one will talk to her at breaktime. She is afraid she will never be able to make friends.

If you are a bully, you may not want to stop bullying people. What could be in it for you? But you are curious enough to have picked up this book so perhaps you are aware that something must be wrong if you need to hurt or frighten other people to get what you want or to cope with difficult feelings. So, this book is for bullies too, like Alan:

Alan's mum is a single parent who has to work long hours and he doesn't see much of her. He goes home from school to an empty house. Alan bullies Ivan whose mum picks him up at home time in the family car. Because Alan feels Ivan is getting the attention he would like, he picks on Ivan relentlessly, jeering at him for being 'soft' and a 'mummy's boy'.

Perhaps you are bullied in some situations and a bully in others. This may seem strange, but it happens quite often. It did to Colm:

Colm is bullied at home by his big brother. Not being able to stand up for himself against his brother makes Colm feel weak. He tries to make himself feel powerful again by bullying smaller children at school.

Perhaps you are neither bullied nor a bully, but you find it difficult and confusing to see other people bullying or being bullied. What should you do? It happened to Tara:

Tara's friend Rebecca is being picked on at school by a gang of spiteful girls who hit her and spoil her things. Tara is torn in two. She wants to help Rebecca, but if she does will the gang turn on her too?

PART ONE

What is Bullying?

WHAT IS BULLYING?

Bullying is about using aggression intentionally to hurt someone. Being aggressive means behaving in a hostile manner towards someone. It is a way of being cruel to another person. It might involve:

- pushing someone or hitting them;
- stealing or breaking someone's things;
- calling someone names;
- sending someone threatening messages by text or email;
- making fun of someone in a nasty way;
- frightening someone into doing things they don't want to do;

3

- leaving someone out of group activities;
- deliberately ignoring someone;
- using chat rooms to spread rumours or lies about someone.

These are just some examples. Unfortunately, bullies know lots more horrible ways to bully apart from these.

Sometimes it will be very obvious to you that you are being bullied, as it was to Sophie:

As Sophie walked out of the school gates, Robert and Matthew grabbed her school bag, emptied her things out onto the pavement and then stamped on them and kicked them around. 'We'll do this again tomorrow unless you give us your lunch money,' said Matthew, 'and if you tell anyone, you'll be very sorry.'

But sometimes the person doing the bullying is someone who cares about you. This kind of bullying can be confusing and hard to recognise. This is what happened to Mala:

Mala's family has just moved to a smart new neighbourhood and Mala is missing her friends. 'What

are you moping about?' her dad asks her. 'You look
like a wet weekend.'

'I miss Laura and Margaret,' Mala tells him.

'You're such an ungrateful girl,' fumes her dad. 'I
spend all this money so that you can move to this
beautiful house and all you do is droop about
looking miserable because you can't see those two
no-hopers.'

Perhaps Mala does feel pleased and excited to be in a
beautiful house, but she also feels sad that she can no
longer see her friends. Her dad cannot cope with
Mala's sad feelings so he is impatient and unkind – a bit
of a bully. The next time Mala feels sad about
something that is important to her, she may try to hide
it from her dad. It's bad enough feeling sad about
something without also being told off for it!

TYPES OF BULLYING

Broadly speaking there are four kinds of bullying and
the aggression used in each kind can involve physical
violence, verbal bullying, psychological intimidation
and/or social rejection.

Physical Bullying

Physical means to do with the body, so physical bullying means that a bully attacks someone's body by, say, pulling their hair or punching them or tripping them up.

Michael isn't good at football. He's small for his age and he finds it hard to control the ball. He always gets picked last for the team. The other boys make fun of him, banging into him 'accidentally' and tripping him up when the games teacher isn't looking. Michael's mum wonders why he's always covered with bruises, but Michael won't say.

If you watch small children playing together you will notice that they tend to grab things off each other or push each other if they have disagreements. As they get older, most children learn to settle arguments by discussion rather than by pushing or hurting the person they are having an argument with. Learning to use words rather than fists is part of growing up.

Unfortunately, some people go on using physical aggression – punching, hitting, slapping, hair-pulling, fighting – as a means of trying to sort out arguments or get their own way. Such bullies almost always pick on or beat up people who are smaller or weaker than they are, or less good at fighting. Because these bullies use physical violence a lot to get their own way, they are often very good fighters.

LEARNING TO USE WORDS RATHER THAN FISTS
IS PART OF GROWING UP

Verbal Bullying

Verbal means using words. Verbal bullying is when a bully hurts or frightens someone by, say, calling them names or making them look silly.

Jane's classmates think that wearing the 'right' label clothing is very important, from trainers to T-shirts. Jane's mum knows how important it is to Jane to have

7

the 'right' label so that she can be dressed like everyone else, but they are just too expensive. Jane's classmates start to make fun of her: 'What a fleabag! Where did you get that coat? The Oxfam shop?'

Jane wishes she didn't have to go to school; she is beginning to dread each new day.

Some adults think that verbal bullying isn't serious because they can't *see* any damage. If a bully hit you and made your nose bleed, people would find that hurt easy to understand. But if you tell them that a bully called you a fleabag, they might just laugh and tell you not to be so sensitive or 'such a baby'.

Of course, words are used a lot when people are teased and it's important not to be oversensitive about teasing (see section on teasing opposite), but verbal bullying is not the same as teasing. Verbal bullying is both cruel and one-sided and it can make you feel small, stupid, unattractive, weak or uncool. If your confidence is knocked in this horrible way, you might even begin to imagine that there must be something wrong with you if this is how you are treated. But no one deserves to be treated cruelly.

There is an old saying:

> *Sticks and stones may break my bones,*
> *but names can never hurt me.*

This is not true.

Name-calling and other kinds of verbal bullying can hurt very much indeed and adults should take them seriously. One girl who was bullied physically and verbally pointed out that, 'Physical hurts heal much more quickly than being called names'.

If you have been bullied in this way, you may find that people say, 'Oh, it's just a bit of teasing. You should be able to take that. Perhaps you've got no sense of humour!'

In fact, there are important differences between verbal bullying and teasing that you should be clear about.

When you are being teased:

- someone is making fun of you in a good-humoured way, and you feel free to make fun back. ('You must have swallowed a calculator to be that good at maths!')
- often the person doing the teasing is someone who knows you well and cares about you, like your mum or your granddad.
- it is not something to be taken seriously – usually you'll find it funny too.
- if you want it to stop, you can ask and the teaser will stop.
- if you do feel upset by teasing, it's a mild feeling that soon goes away.

9

- it's a two-way thing – someone who teases will also get teased and someone who is teased will also tease a person back.

When teasing becomes cruel and causes someone distress, it has slipped over the dividing line between teasing and bullying and become verbal bullying. When teasing becomes one-sided and the same person is always at the receiving end, then teasing has become verbal bullying. Often of course, bullies use a mixture of physical and verbal aggression.

Name-calling
Verbal bullying is often done by name-calling. This is usually about people's appearance and might include names such as 'fatty', 'spotty' and 'four-eyes'. References to the way people are perceived might include names such as 'swot', 'thicko' and 'snob'. And while assigning nicknames is sometimes something that can be humorous, playful or affectionate (as in 'Becks' for David Beckham), the experience can be an upsetting one when it teeters over the edge of harmless banter and becomes a way of mocking someone's appearance or personality. Your very identity can feel under attack.

Racist Name-calling and Bullying

Children from ethnic minorities (black, Asian, traveller or other minorities) are often victims of racist name-calling and other kinds of bullying. If there are only a few children from ethnic minorities in a school or neighbourhood they may suffer more racial abuse than those who live in communities where their ethnic group is well represented. Some schools have successfully used a mentoring programme – this means asking older children to befriend and help minority children who feel alone or who are being bullied. They also have assemblies which talk about the problem of racism as part of their anti-bullying strategies. In this way the children who do the racist name-calling are helped to understand the hurt and offence they cause. Such programmes also give the victims help and support.

Sexual Name-calling and Bullying

Sexual name-calling is now more widespread than it used to be and it can be particularly difficult to bear because young people reaching puberty can feel very self-conscious about their bodies and about what kind of young man or young woman they are going to be. Sometimes girls can be labelled as 'slags', 'slappers' or 'tarts'. Perhaps some of the boys who use these words are embarrassed about their own developing and changing bodies and feelings of attraction towards girls and they try – in this horrible, bullying way – to make themselves feel confident and worldly, or to show off to other people. Perhaps some of the girls who use these words about other girls are also expressing their own anxieties about their bodies and growing up by putting down others in this cruel fashion.

Homophobic Name-calling and Bullying

Being gay means that you feel attracted towards someone of the same sex rather than someone of the opposite sex. Homophobic bullying (the bullying of gay people) is particularly difficult for young people who think they might be gay. Very often such young people already feel isolated – they may not have told their parents that they are gay and they may not feel able to talk to their teachers or friends through fear of embarrassment. When young people are trying to work out who they are, such bullying can be very damaging. Few young gay people dare to come out (let others know they are gay) at school. Those who do often suffer terrible bullying. While few teachers these days will tolerate racist or sexist name-calling or bullying, they do not always take into account bullying related to being gay, despite government guidelines advising that the issue should be addressed.

Homophobic name-calling is not just directed at young

people who *are* gay, but also at people who do not fit a very narrow view of what boys and girls 'should' do and like – for example, boys who enjoy chatting to girls or who are good at art, and girls who play football or don't dress in a girlie way. 'Gay' is sometimes used as a term of negativity (for example, 'This film is so gay'), even in primary schools where younger children often do not know what it means. What they do learn, however, is that 'gay' seems to be something with which it is not good to be associated. Young people who are experiencing this kind of bullying may not seek help because they feel embarrassed or they think adults won't take it seriously.

If you are being taunted and jeered at by bullies, it can be very hard to bear, and verbal abuse can sometimes be more painful and difficult to deal with than physical abuse. Turn to Part Two to find out more on sticking up for yourself and to remind you of all the good things about yourself. Part Four will discuss tactics to deal with verbal bullying.

Psychological Bullying

This can be a subtle, indirect and less obvious way of hurting or frightening someone, but it can be very powerful. It can be intimidating in a way that can sometimes be difficult to describe to someone else. If you get a nasty text message, for example, you are not being physically hurt by the bully or called something horrible to your face, but all the same you may feel very shaken and hurt deep inside yourself. This is a kind of bullying that can sometimes be hard to recognise.

Bullies can sometimes use words or actions in such a way that you feel controlled or trapped. It's as though there is no way out.

Bernadette was sitting on a bench in the park when a girl came up to her and said, 'That's my bench.' When Bernadette moved and sat on another bench, the girl came up to her again and said the same thing. Bernadette felt so foolish, uncomfortable and scared that she left the park.

YOU MAY FEEL VERY SHAKEN AND HURT DEEP
INSIDE YOURSELF

Cyber-bullying

Cyber-bullying is bullying behaviour that misuses technology to send or post insults or rumours about someone by email, text, phone, instant messaging or in chatrooms. It can include photographing or filming people in private or embarrassing situations and then putting the photograph or video up on the internet.

Marc started receiving nasty text messages. Then he discovered that more nasty messages about him had also been posted in a chatroom on the web. Marc didn't feel safe any more. It was as though he couldn't escape the bullies even in his own home.

'Friendships' formed on social networking sites or in chatrooms can happen very quickly and easily largely because they are not real. It can be hard to remember that, unless you also know the person you are chatting to in real life, these cyber relationships are based on fantasy – you don't actually know the person you are talking to and they may not be trustworthy. Children who are lonely or shy can be particularly vulnerable when social networking site or chatroom friendships go wrong because they can become very emotionally involved in them. And even confident young people can be shocked and hurt when a cyber-'friend' turns into a cyber-bully.

Online bullying can be particularly disturbing and upsetting because the internet is a public forum. It is also possible, given the nature of social networking sites, for other people to add their own insulting and hurtful comments to what has been written.

As with group bullying where it is possible for group members not to feel directly responsible for what is happening, cyber-bullying can feel anonymous. As there is no face-to-face contact with the victim, cyber-bullies can sometimes feel free to be more vindictive and cruel than they would dare to be in person. They don't see the impact on their victims and they imagine they won't have to deal with the consequences. Fortunately, it is now much more possible to trace cyber-bullies and there are things that can be done to make them stop (see page 108).

Cyber-bullying is very disturbing because it can leave you feeling unsafe, exposed and worried about who you can trust.

Social Bullying
Bullies do this by intimidating or convincing a class or group to ignore someone or exclude them from group activities. They might also play horrible tricks on them.

When the teacher asked everyone to choose a partner for project work, no one ever chose John.

Nicole told her friends that anyone who talked to Katy wouldn't be her friend any more.

Denise told Vanessa that if she bought her some sweets she would sit with her at lunchtime. When Vanessa gave her the sweets, Denise sat with her friends and wouldn't let Vanessa join them.

It can be particularly hard to feel OK about yourself if you are treated like this because no one in the class or group takes your side or tries to help. It can leave you feeling very lonely and hurt.

Bullying Yourself

Sometimes you can start to imagine that bullying must be happening to you because you're not the 'right kind' of person. This is not so! This is one more kind of bullying. This kind is not something that happens to you from the outside. It comes from *inside* you. It's bullying yourself.

This may sound like an odd idea. 'People don't bully themselves!' you're probably saying. But lots of people do just that although they are often not aware that what they are doing to themselves is a kind of bullying. So far this book has talked about the nasty things that other people can do to you. But perhaps sometimes there can be a bullying voice inside you that tells you that whatever has happened is all your fault because you're such an awful person. Or the bullying voice may tell you it's not surprising that no one wants to be your friend because you're not good enough to be anyone's friend. This is what happened to Tabitha:

Tabitha arranged to go swimming on Saturday with her friend Jane. She got to the pool on time, but Jane didn't show up. After a while, Tabitha began to think: 'Jane probably hasn't come because she doesn't really like me. I expect she thinks I'm awful. She probably doesn't want anyone from school to see us together.' (In fact, Jane had missed the bus. She turned up a short while later full of apologies for being late.)

The bullying voice inside Tabitha was really attacking her! This kind of inside bullying is horrible and very painful to bear. Why should Tabitha have to put up with the disappointment of Jane not being there as arranged *and* have to bully herself by thinking that it's because she, Tabitha, has something wrong with her?

People who bully themselves often do so because they have trouble finding good ways of thinking about mistakes and disappointments. Perhaps you've been told that if you don't get something right first time, there is something wrong with you or it's your fault (you didn't work hard enough, etc). In fact, mistakes and disappointments are bound to happen in life because there are lots of things we can't know without learning about them and things we can't do until we have been taught or until we have practised. You can't ride a bike, for example, unless you learn how to balance and that usually means falling off at first until you get the hang of it! The mistakes you make are important because they tell you where you went wrong and how to do it better next time.

If you have a bullying voice inside you it can be difficult to get rid of it because it is a part of you and it can pop up unexpectedly, particularly when things are difficult for you. Perhaps, though, you can try fighting back by reminding yourself of all the good things about you. If you have a bullying voice you'd like to get rid of you may find some of the Happiness Workouts in Part Three of this book useful.

BULLYING YOURSELF

HOW DO BULLIES GET AWAY WITH IT?

Children who are bullies often get away with bullying because they are careful to hide what they are doing from adults who would stop them. They also rely on the people they bully and on other children who know what is going on to remain silent about it.

HOW MUCH BULLYING IS THERE?

People can come across bullying in all kinds of situations where power, aggression, will and strength are tested out. It can happen to people of every age. Children may be bullied in schools by other children or by teachers, or they may be bullied in public places – for example, going to and from school or in the park. Adults are often better equipped than children to confront or avoid such aggression, but they too can be on the receiving end of bullying, at work and in institutions such as old people's homes, prisons or the armed services. Bullying may also take place in the home where parents may bully each other, children or elderly family members. Siblings (brothers and sisters) may bully each other.

ChildLine is a twenty-four-hour national telephone helpline for children in trouble or danger (see **Where to Get Help and Advice** at the back of the book). ChildLine researchers recently conducted a survey of bullying in schools and found that 'bullying in schools is commonplace, even in schools with anti-bullying policies in place: sixty-four per cent of primary school children and forty-five per cent of secondary children said they had been bullied at some point in their schools. Half (fifty per cent) of the primary school children and more than one in four (twenty-seven per cent) of the secondary children responding said they had been bullied in the last year'. The ChildLine survey found that equal numbers of boys and girls were bullied at primary school, but that more girls than boys were bullied in secondary school.

The ChildLine survey also found that eighteen per cent of primary and twenty-five per cent of secondary children admitted bullying others during the previous year. As children who bully are often reluctant to admit that they are bullies, it is likely that these figures do not reflect the true level of bullying, and that it is really much higher.

Children who phoned the ChildLine Bullying Line were asked how long bullying had been going on. Forty-eight per cent of these children had been bullied for over a month and up to a year. Twenty-two per cent of callers had been bullied for over one year and three per cent described bullying which had persisted for more than five years. Twenty-seven per cent had been bullied less than a month.

ChildLine stated that the number of children reporting that they had been bullied had risen to record levels, but this increase may indicate that more children are willing to ask for help rather than that bullying is on the increase. Encouragingly, three out of five parents whose children admitted being bullied said they felt the school dealt with the problem effectively.

Research into cyber-bullying in the United States has found that more than one in three young people have experienced cyber-bullying online and over twenty-five per cent of teenagers have been bullied repeatedly through their mobile phones or on the internet.

WHERE DOES BULLYING TAKE PLACE?

Most cases of bullying take place at school – indeed, one researcher found that one-fifth of children are bullied at some point in their school life. But bullying can also take place going to and from school; some of the most violent cases of bullying have happened at this time when adults are not there to supervise. These incidents can involve children from the same school or from other schools. And, of course, bullying can take place away from school altogether. You can also be vulnerable to cyber-bullying on the internet or on your phone.

Bullying at School

Most schools now have an anti-bullying policy so that everyone in the school is aware that bullying is not acceptable and that such behaviour will be challenged. When a school anti-bullying policy is drawn up, safety going to and from school must also be considered.

While head teachers are not legally responsible for preventing bullying outside their schools, the Department for Education says that they should take steps to tackle it. It advises that schools seek police presence at trouble spots where necessary and talk to the heads of other schools to see if they think pupils are being bullied off the premises.

Bullying at Boarding School

In the past, some people believed that bullying in boarding schools was good for pupils and prepared them for the 'real world'. Boarding schools used to have fagging (where new pupils had to do chores for older pupils) and even prefects were even allowed to beat and punish young pupils. These days corporal punishment (being beaten or hit) is illegal in all schools in the UK, including boarding schools.

People at boarding school are usually more closely supervised by teachers and other staff than children at day schools. This can sometimes help to stop bullying taking place. On the other hand, if bullying is taking place, it can be very difficult for the victims of bullying to escape because there is nowhere to escape to – no safe place where the bullies cannot find them. Sometimes boarding school pupils cannot even feel safe at night if there are bullies in their dormitory. Boarding school children have reported quite serious assaults taking place in dormitories at night and at the weekends, sometimes carried out by older children who are monitors or prefects.

Bullying at Home

Bullying can also be carried out in the home – by brothers and sisters and by parents. Sometimes children are so used to being treated in a bullying way in their home that they don't even realise that they are being bullied. It is difficult for people brought up in such homes to believe that hostile and aggressive ways of treating others are not normal or acceptable. It is possible that some children who bully others at school do so because they, in turn, are bullied at home.

WHO ARE THE PEOPLE WHO ARE BULLIED?

'We had a supply teacher who couldn't keep order. I felt sorry for her – my class gave her such a bad time. She looked as if she was going to cry sometimes. But I didn't dare not join in.' Jonathan (12)

'At my last school I was frequently beaten up because I am gay. It was terrible. No one bothered to help me. Teachers just stood there and did nothing.' Chris (14)

'My stammer gets worse when people take the mickey; there's always the odd one that does it.'
Annie (8)

'Someone created a webpage about me and said all sorts of mean and weird things that weren't true. Then other people started adding their comments – all horrible too. I couldn't face going back to school because I didn't know who had done it.'
Asher (13)

'I'm the only Asian girl in my class. The others have started calling me Paki and making fun of the things I bring to eat at lunchtime.' Pria (14)

'When I was little I was attacked by a dog. I have a jagged scar across my lip. People at school call me "scarface". What does it matter what you look like? It's what is underneath that counts.' Jamie (9)

People who are bullied often do not know how to defend themselves from being trampled on by other people. Perhaps they are afraid to stick up for themselves. Sometimes they even trample on themselves by allowing a bullying and criticising voice inside themselves to attack them.

People who are bullied are often pleasant, thoughtful and friendly, but they can also often be described as:

shy   timid   afraid
unassertive   dependent
lacking in confidence   lacking in self-esteem

People who are bullied allow others to control them. They often imagine that it must be their fault that they are being bullied – they think they must be a weak person who has brought it on themselves.

People who are bullied often have something that sets them apart from the rest or makes them stand out. Research shows that bullies like to pick on:

- people who don't feel good about themselves and who find it hard to make friends. These are usually people who don't look confident and happy or people who are isolated.
- people who are smaller, weaker or younger than they are.
- new kids – people who change schools and people who transfer from primary to secondary school are often at risk of bullying.
- people who are clumsy or bad at sports. These are the people who always get picked last for the team.
- people whose bodies are beginning, due to puberty,

to change and develop into adult bodies, or people who are 'late developers' and whose bodies haven't yet begun to change and develop. It's easy for bullies to make people feel self-conscious or 'abnormal' at this point in their lives.

- people who are plump or fat.
- people who wear glasses; have a stammer; wear braces; have a hearing aid; have big ears; have red hair; use a wheelchair or are in some other way physically different to the majority.
- people with learning difficulties.
- people who have a different skin colour; cultural background; regional accent; religion or class.
- people who have a different sexual orientation to the majority. They may be homosexual (gay or lesbian) or bisexual.
- people whose parents are rich and have lots of nice things, or, at the other extreme, people whose parents are poor and who have few nice things.
- people who may be envied because they are good-looking or have lots of friends or are very intelligent.
- people who are in the wrong place at the wrong time. For example, the unlucky person who finds her/ himself alone in the toilets when the bullies walk in.

- people whose parents or other family members are a focus of public attention – perhaps their dad is in prison or their mum is a member of parliament.

Of course, if any of these apply to you, you won't necessarily be bullied. Perhaps none of these apply to you and you *are* being bullied – sometimes bullying can happen for no apparent reason.

YOU'RE NOT THE ONLY ONE
Bullying is not something new although these days it is, perhaps, something that is more recognised. Here are

some examples of well known people who were bullied as children:

- Hollywood star Tom Cruise, who is dyslexic, was lonely and the target of cruel jokes. He said, 'That experience made me tough inside, because you learn to accept ridicule.'
- Comedian David Walliams drew on his own experience of being bullied at school as an eleven-year-old when writing his children's book, *Billionaire Boy*. 'In the book there is a cross-country run and if you're one of the fat kids at the back the other kids would have changed by the time you turned up and they would jeer at you when you crossed the finish line. That happened to me.'
- Rap star and producer Eminem was so badly bullied that he attempted suicide. He also spent five days in a coma after a violent attack. Later he wrote a song about this experience called 'Brain Damage'.
- According to his biographer Jonathan Dimbleby, Prince Charles was bullied at his school because he was heir to the throne.
- Polar explorer Sir Ranulph Fiennes has described being bullied at Eton, Britain's best known public school. Fiennes used to cry hopelessly in bed and think about killing himself by jumping off a bridge

into the Thames. Fortunately his mother believed him when he told her what was happening.

WHO ARE THE BULLIES?

'I got told off for bullying Emma, but she wears a cardigan with stupid rabbit buttons and her mum always kisses her goodbye at the school gate. She's such a baby! I've been walking to school on my own for ages.' Tracy (9)

'Jasyn thinks he's so great with his iPod and his new trainers. Me and Tony started texting him, saying he was going to be beaten up. That soon took the smile off his face.' Kevin (11)

'My gang has all the cool lads in it. We always sit at the back of the class. When a new boy with a Yorkshire accent tried to sit with us we all started imitating him and he soon got the message he wasn't wanted.' Max (12)

There have been lots of ideas put forward by psychologists (people who study human behaviour) and others to try and explain why people bully. There is probably more than one reason for bullying behaviour and these reasons may be linked in some way.

People who bully aren't much fun to have around. They can be described as:

**aggressive   mean   insensitive
cruel   controlling   lacking in empathy**

More about bullies:

- Bullies think that getting their own way by being hurtful, aggressive or frightening is OK or the only possible way.
- Bullies are often thought of as stupid people who only manage to get what they want by picking on those smaller than themselves. This is not always the case:
  - Some bullies are very clever people who terrorise others by making fun of them, jeering at them and putting pressure on them.
  - Some bullies are very clever at pretending to be friends, gaining your confidence and then spreading malicious stories about you.
- Bullies can be found in every kind of school, from nursery to secondary, from state to private schools.
- Both boys and girls can be bullies.
- Bullies sometimes bully people who are younger than they are, but many also bully people their own age or older.

- Girl bullies usually prefer to use verbal bullying and pranks rather than physical bullying, but not always. Girl bullies will often isolate their victim from the rest of the group and make other people ignore them. They might try to exclude them from playground games, for example.
- Physical bullying and threats are more common among boy bullies, but not always.
- Some bullies like to organise themselves into groups and plan attacks – physical, verbal and psychological – on victims.
- Some bullies use threats or force to make people give them money, sweets or other items that they want. This is called extortion (forcing someone to give you something against their will).

Adult Bullies

Some adults, teachers for example, are bullies. They use their authority to make cruel personal remarks ('Isn't it time you lost some weight, lad?'), unfair comparisons ('It's clear that your sister inherited the brains, not you'), threats and (rarely, but it does happen) physical assaults. It is illegal for teachers to use corporal punishment (hitting, smacking or physical assault of any kind). Some parents are bullies and this can be very hard as you feel you have no escape and no one to turn to. If this is the case, you might want to call one of the helplines listed at the end of this book.

Group Bullying

When bullying is done by a group of bullies rather than by one individual, it can be particularly difficult for the victim of the bullying to deal with, because she or he will experience rejection and hurt by a whole group of hostile people rather than just one person. It is also frightening to be one person against a group.

WHY DO BULLIES DO IT?

Here are some of the reasons bullies feel they need to bully:

- It is not uncommon for children who are bullied at home by their parents or older brothers and sisters, to themselves use bullying behaviour at school. Hurting someone else rather than being the one who is hurt is a way of helping themselves to feel better.
- Sometimes bullies have something very sad or distressing or difficult happening in another area of their life (perhaps their gran is ill or their dad has lost his job) and they try to hide their feelings about this and regain some control by bullying.

- Some children who bully may not yet understand that other people have feelings and that what they are doing is causing hurt and harm. They have difficulty seeing things from another person's point of view or understanding their feelings. They may believe that they are just messing about or having a laugh.
- People who bully are sometimes afraid of people who are different from them – they want others to be the same in order to feel safe and secure. Sometimes bullies are afraid that *they* are different from other people and this difference will not be liked.
- Sometimes people who are angry and upset about something and find it difficult to cope with these painful feelings will try to get rid of them by picking on someone else. One of the reasons that many bullies are so good at knowing when other people are feeling frightened or weak is that they are themselves frightened and vulnerable people underneath their 'hard' front. They see in others the weakness or fear they pretend they don't have.
- Some people bully because they just don't know any good ways of getting on with other people. Perhaps their parents fight when they have disagreements instead of discussing them and working them out. When adults do this, it's not

surprising that it's difficult for a child to learn how to get on with others without fighting and bullying.

- Some people bully because they are envious – someone else has something they long to have.
- Some people bully because they lack self-confidence. If they can control other people by bullying them, this helps them to feel more powerful, confident and secure.

THE IMPACT OF BULLYING

An American teenager, Megan Meier, hanged herself three weeks before her fourteeth birthday. An investigation discovered that she had been the victim of cyber-bullying through a social networking site. A former friend's mother created a false account pretending to be a boy called Josh. Megan began to correspond with 'Josh' but once her trust had been won, was sent messages full of hate. According to her father, the final message before she killed herself read: 'You are a bad person and everybody hates you. Have a bad rest of your life. The world would be a better place without you.' As a result of this shocking case, a law was introduced in the US to prohibit abusive communication by any means, including the internet.

'I don't want to die, but going on like this is a living hell.' Thirteen-year-old Hirofumi Shikagawa, left this note before hanging himself in a bathroom in Japan. He had been bullied at school by his classmates. This shocking case was taken up by the Japanese press.

Sixteen-year-old Katharine Bamber was found hanged in the garage of her home. In her suicide note she wrote: *'I hate my life . . . People like **** make it hell. I hate them for threatening me and calling me a tart and a slag. I can't take it any more. I'm very scared and hurt inside by them and the only way I know out is by killing myself.'*

The scale of homophobic bullying was highlighted when seven US teenagers who were gay committed suicide following homophobic abuse. The 'It Gets Better' video campaign was launched in reaction to these deaths and received enormous support, from Barack Obama amongst many others.

One of thirteen-year-old Amy Louise Paul's friends turned against her and set up a group on the internet called 'We hate Amy Louise – for all those people who hope she would die already' and invited others at school to join. Many did, adding cruel and spiteful *comments. Amy Louise was very hurt that someone who had been a friend could treat her this way and not surprisingly, she became withdrawn and distressed.*

Thirteen-year-old Bangladeshi pupil, Ahmed Iqbal Ullah, was stabbed to death in the playground at Burnage High School, Manchester. His killer was a white boy who regularly bullied Asian children. The enquiry which reported on the killing was highly critical of the school's mismanagement of racist behaviour.

The impact of bullying can be very serious indeed, and can even result in some children harming themselves. In such cases as these, bullying is probably not the only factor that has led these young people to harm themselves, but it is believed to have contributed significantly to their despair. If you have ever felt so awful that you have considered harming yourself it is important that you seek help. See **Where to Get Help and Advice** at the end of this book.

Other children who are bullied dread going to school and often pretend to be ill, run away from home, refuse to go to school any more or become seriously depressed. Others may turn to alcohol or drugs as a way of blotting out painful feelings. Some even turn to crime, perhaps hoping that if they are, say, caught shop-lifting, the grown-ups around will realise that something is wrong elsewhere in their lives.

Bullying can cause so much pain and distress that some people who have been bullied are affected by it for the rest of their lives – not surprisingly, they find it hard to trust anyone ever again and they have difficulty making friends and forming relationships. They may grow up to be insecure, frightened and anxious people who perceive this situation as their fault. Alternatively, they may start using aggressive and violent ways of behaving in the hope that this will keep them safe.

WHY IT'S NOT GOOD TO BE A BULLY

Novelist Jilly Cooper was a bully at her girls' public school: 'We bullied Jennifer because she was fat and Enid because she had large breasts at eleven years old. It was not considered right to be so over-endowed. Our worst bullying, however, was reserved for our under-housemistress, Miss Harris. We cornered her and stripped off her clothes down to her petticoat. As a punishment we were denied sandwiches at tea.'

When bullies get away with behaving badly they start believing that rules do not apply to them. They think they can behave aggressively and no one will stop them. They may get away with this as children if there is no adult intervention, but their development can be damaged. They may have difficulty as grown-ups with fitting into society and difficulty in distinguishing between right and wrong. They may also find it quite confusing when they discover that people do not like their bullying ways because they have no idea what they are doing wrong.

People who bully risk getting into the habit of using aggression and violence to get their own way and they may never learn how to treat others well. Often people bully because they don't feel safe or they lack confidence and self-esteem. They are not going to have a chance to grow in confidence if they cover up the problem by bullying.

AN ATMOSPHERE OF FEAR

Bullying can also affect other people besides those who are being bullied or who are bullying because bullying creates an atmosphere of fear. People often stand by and watch and do nothing to stop the bullies or help the person who is being bullied. There are many possible reasons for this:

- Even if you are not the person being bullied, it is hard to feel relaxed and happy when you know that someone else is being hurt. You may be afraid to help as it might be your turn next.

- Perhaps you are secretly glad someone else is being hurt because it takes the bullies' attention away from you – although this can also make you feel guilty.

- It's hard to have confidence in the teachers or other adults around if they either don't notice what's going on, or notice, but don't seem able to do anything to stop it or just don't do anything to stop it.

- If the bullies are the adults, you may feel quite despairing. You need to tell an adult you can trust about what is happening. See Part Four for suggestions.

- If your friends are being bullied, you might be frightened to be seen talking to them in the playground in case you are bullied too. At the same time, you'll probably feel ashamed of yourself for not sticking up for them. This is a heavy burden to carry.

- If bullying takes place in the toilets, you will have to plan to go when the bullies are not around. Not very convenient!

- If bullies hang round the school gate at home time, you might have to wait for your friends every day so that you can all leave safely together.

While keeping safe tactics are sensible, it's just not right that you have to tiptoe around carefully all the time in order to keep the bullies at bay. It's also not right that bullies can frighten you enough to stop you sticking up for your friends. Why should the bullies get away with it?

WHAT CAN BE DONE?

It is painful to be bullied. It is painful to be a bully.

Things don't have to go on being like this for you, whether you are a bully or someone who is bullied.

Some children who have been bullied have found ways of helping themselves. When Oli Watts was sixteen he was bullied remorselessly at his school because he wasn't born locally. He felt as though he was 'on a desert island'. He said, 'I was left with a broken character. I was an empty shell.' When he was nineteen, Oli published his story on the internet and started a website where children who are bullied can tell their stories and offer advice. See **Where to Get Help and Advice** at the end of this book for information about this and other resources.

It is possible to find a different, happy way to be with people and to get along with people. Reading this book can be the start of your search to find this different, happy way.

PART TWO

Sticking Up for Yourself

CHANGING HOW YOU FEEL ABOUT YOURSELF

To stop being bullied or to stop being a bully, things need to change for you in your inner world as well as in the outside world. The idea of having an inner world may be new to you – it means the private and personal space inside you where you have your own thoughts and feelings that other people do not know about. Outside world changes you can make are discussed in Part Four of this book. These changes tend to be of a practical kind and are to do with learning self-protection and strategies to stop bullying.

Making changes to your inside world is more difficult and takes longer because it involves changing the way you feel about yourself and how you deserve to be treated. One example of such a change that has already been mentioned in Part One is the possibility of getting rid of the bullying and critical voice inside you that can tell you it's your fault when you are badly treated.

STICKING UP FOR YOURSELF

As mentioned before, people who are bullied often imagine that it must be their fault that they are being bullied – that they must be a weak person who has brought it on themselves. If you feel small and weak this can make you less likely to tell someone about the bullying as you may think that having to ask for help *proves* that you are weak. In fact, you have simply not been helped to learn how to stick up for yourself.

People who are bullies often behave in this horrible way because, underneath all the swaggering and the aggression, they lack self-confidence. If they can control other people by frightening or hurting them, this helps them to feel more powerful, confident and secure. They have not been helped to learn how to stick up for themselves either!

Here is what happened to Niti and Mark:

Niti's class is in the middle of a spelling test when the boy sitting next to her, Jason, asks in a whisper how to spell 'acknowledge'. Their teacher, Mr Greenacre, does not allow people to help each other in tests so Niti just shakes her head at Jason. Suddenly Mr Greenacre shouts out, 'Niti, I saw you helping Jason. No marks at all for either of you.' Niti tries to explain that she didn't say anything, but Mr Greenacre won't listen. Jason doesn't say a word. After the class, Niti talks to her friend, Sonia, about it. 'It's really unfair,' says Sonia, 'you weren't breaking any rules. You should have stuck up for yourself!'

When Mark gets to school, he sees Peter in tears – Peter's cat died that morning. This reminds Mark of how he felt when his dad had his pet rabbit put down because they weren't allowed to keep pets any more by the landlord. To shut out these painful feelings, Mark starts making fun of Peter: 'What a cry-baby! Did diddums's catty-watty kick the bucket, then?'

Mark doesn't know that it's OK to feel upset and angry about the dreadful thing that happened to his rabbit; he needs to stick up for himself by finding a better way of dealing with these feelings – a way that doesn't hurt someone else.

Both Niti and Mark need to stick up for themselves. So, how do you learn to stick up for yourself?

If you want to stop being bullied or if you want to stop being a bully you need help from someone who will always be on your side; someone you can rely on. That 'someone' is you.

No one knows better than Niti and Mark that what happened wasn't their fault: Niti didn't break the class rule. Mark didn't deserve to have his rabbit put down and his grief at losing his pet ignored.

Niti and Mark can begin to stick up for themselves by keeping this in mind when the adults either won't listen or won't understand how difficult and painful the situation is.

RELYING ON YOURSELF

Of course, this is just the beginning. Niti and Mark may want to stick up for themselves by speaking up for themselves. Speaking up for yourself can be a hard thing to do if you aren't confident about your own good qualities and your own strength. After all, how will you feel if you speak up for yourself and it doesn't work? Perhaps Mr Greenacre will still refuse to listen; Mark's dad may tell him not to be such a baby about the rabbit. Things won't always go your way however unfair it is.

When this happens, what you need is to feel secure and confident inside that you like yourself and that you understand how things really are. Even if Mr Greenacre won't listen or won't believe her, Niti knows that she didn't break a rule and that what happened wasn't fair. Even if Mark's dad doesn't understand how Mark feels about his rabbit, Mark knows how precious his pet was to him, how cruel it was that it had to be put down and how angry and upset he is about it. Like Niti and Mark, you will often need to be your own good friend on whom you can rely to understand how things really are for you, even if no one else does.

Learning to stick up for yourself isn't something that happens overnight. Any kind of change in the way you think about yourself and in the way you behave takes time. So, stick with it.

LEARNING TO FEEL SECURE AND CONFIDENT INSIDE

To feel good about yourself inside doesn't mean that you have to be:

- physically stronger than everyone else;
- cleverer than everyone else;
- the same as everyone else;
- richer than everyone else;
- able to make people do what you want.

The kind of power that feeling good about yourself gives you is personal to you. It doesn't depend on comparisons with other people.

This is the inner power that will begin to grow and eventually enable you to stick up for yourself when other people try to bully you. If you find yourself wanting to bully someone else, your inner power will help you find a better way of coping with difficult feelings.

Inner power can become part of you and stay with you all your life. And it will keep on coming in handy. Bullying can happen in adulthood too!

To feel secure and confident inside yourself:

- understand your feelings;
- be responsible for your feelings;
- be responsible for your behaviour;
- develop and use your inner power.

Understanding Your Feelings

Excitement   Anger   Rage
Depression   Curiosity   Terror   Joy
Pleasure   Fear   Anxiety   Humiliation
Surprise   Contempt   Enjoyment   Shame
Fury   Boredom   Loneliness   Aggression
Astonishment   Jealousy   Frustration
Delight   Impatience   Sadness   Pain
Tension   Irritation   Friendship
Affection   Restlessness

These words describe feelings that we all have. (You'll be able to think of others not listed here.)

What Are Feelings For?

Your feelings tell you what is going on inside you. It's normal to have feelings and it's normal to have all of them or some of them at different times.

Are Some Feelings Bad?

Feelings aren't 'good' or 'bad' – feelings just are.

Quite a lot of people are confused about this – they imagine that if you feel rage with someone you might actually harm that person or if you envy someone, you might actually do them down in some way. This is not so – feelings cannot hurt anyone.

People choose whether or not their feelings lead to actions and whether these actions are good or bad:

Annette feels angry because John has borrowed her bike without asking. She chooses to hit him and pull his hair.

Sam feels angry because Joe spilt water all over his painting. He chooses to tell him how angry he feels that his work has been spoilt.

Winston feels angry because Paulette is making fun of him. He chooses not to show how angry he is.

Anger

Anger is the feeling that most frightens people so they often pretend to themselves that they don't feel any. They think anger is a 'bad' feeling to have. In fact, anger is an important feeling that should be listened to – anger tells you lots of useful things about yourself.

1. Anger tells you how you want to be treated (because not being well treated makes you feel angry).

This is what happened to Jennifer:

Jennifer had a bad day at school. Her teacher told her he 'hadn't got round' to looking at the story that she'd spent such a lot of time on when he'd promised to talk to her about it that day. He then told her to clear up a mess she didn't make. That evening Jennifer told her mum about it: 'I feel like killing Mr Thomas!' she said crossly. 'Jennifer!' said Mum, 'What an awful thing to say. It won't do to have violent feelings and especially not from a girl.'

'I FEEL LIKE KILLING MR THOMAS !'

Quite rightly, Jennifer feels angry because she wasn't well treated at school by Mr Thomas. She wants to let her mum know how cross and disappointed she feels, but her mum is someone who is frightened of hearing about angry feelings. Instead of being able to talk about them with Jennifer, she tells her off for having such feelings.

Mum is also not as surprised or disapproving when Jennifer's brother expresses angry feelings, as though it's all right for boys, but not for girls. In fact, both girls and boys have angry, aggressive feelings (and, of course, both girls and boys have tender, caring feelings too).

Unfortunately, parents sometimes find it hard to accept and think about their own difficult feelings, let alone their children's. They can't think about such feelings as anger, aggression and rage with you and can't try to help you to understand them because it's something they have not managed for themselves. This can be very disappointing and frustrating for you when you need someone helpful to talk to. It may be that some grown-ups are put off by language that sounds threatening (like Jennifer saying she wants to 'kill' Mr Thomas) and would find it easier to sympathise if you find another way to put it. But keep trying to find a trustworthy adult or older person who is good at talking and thinking about feelings. They do exist!

2. Anger tells you what you think is fair (because unfairness makes you feel angry).

   This is what happened to Bernadette:

   Gabrielle and Bernadette are expected to take turns washing up, but Gabrielle often gets out of her turn because she 'can't be late for Guides'. Today, Bernadette has been invited to a friend's to watch a DVD, but when she asks to leave early Mum refuses to let her. 'You can watch DVDs any old time,' she says. Bernadette feels angry – why can't her mum understand that being invited to see the DVD is important to her? It's also not fair that Gabrielle gets out of the washing up so easily.

   It's very upsetting when a parent seems to approve of what one child chooses to do and not value what another child chooses to do. Perhaps Bernadette can try explaining to her mum how this makes her feel.

3. Anger tells you what you find important (because when things that are important to you are laughed at, or ignored, you feel angry).

   This is what happened to Rupert:

Rupert enjoys pop music, but his parents and his
brother only approve of classical music. If they find
him listening to pop music, they say, 'You can't
really be enjoying that awful noise'.

Perhaps Rupert's family think they are just teasing him, but their rudeness and lack of respect for the things that Rupert enjoys is making it very hard for Rupert to stick up for himself and stay in touch with his feelings of enjoyment about pop music. He feels angry that his family are so dismissive about his preferences – after all, he doesn't make rude remarks about their musical taste.

Your Feelings Belong to You
Some people like to tell other people what they should be thinking or feeling about something or they tell you that it's wrong to feel the way you do about something.

This is a kind of bullying. If someone tries to bully you in this way, you can be your own best friend and stick up for yourself – after all, who can possibly know more about how you feel about something than you?

Your feelings are yours – no one can make you feel something. If you feel glad or if you feel depressed, that's how you feel. And, of course, you are responsible for what you choose to do about that feeling.

It may not always be appropriate to say out loud what you are feeling – it may not be a good idea, for example, to tell your head teacher that she annoys you. Sometimes it's better to be tactful (considerate about other people's feelings) and keep this type of feeling to yourself!

Mixed Feelings

Sometimes it can be confusing to work out your feelings because you have more than one at a time. This is quite normal:

Surprise   Pleasure

Martin feels surprised to be chosen to sing the solo at the school concert and at the same time he feels pleased.

Sometimes, many different feelings come one after the other:

Pleasure   Admiration
Humiliation   Rage

Stephen feels pleased with his new T-shirt so he puts it on and stands in front of the mirror to admire himself.

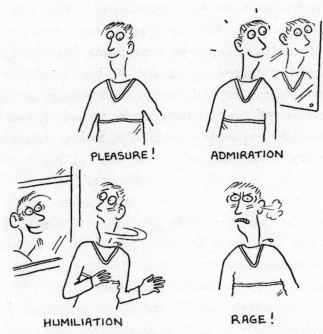

PLEASURE! ADMIRATION

HUMILIATION RAGE!

Suddenly he notices that his brother is looking at him through the window and laughing at him. Stephen feels humiliated that his pleasure in his appearance is being ridiculed. To deal with this painful feeling, he feels rage – how dare Jonathan sneak up on him like that and poke fun!

Talking About Feelings

Feelings are so much part of our lives that you might expect everyone to be good at talking about them.

Sadly, this isn't so. Some people (including lots of adults) are uncomfortable talking about their own feelings and uneasy when they hear other people talking about theirs.

Some people think it's a sign of weakness to talk about feelings. They couldn't be more wrong. In fact, it takes a lot of courage and strength to keep in touch with your feelings and to be able to listen and understand when other people talk about theirs.

Of course, this doesn't mean that you should talk about your feelings to just anyone. You want to be sure that what you are saying will be heard and thought about by someone trustworthy who cares about you. If your parents or the other adults in your life aren't good at talking about feelings, look out for someone who is – perhaps your sister or brother, a friend or your teacher.

Good Ways to Talk About Feelings

If you say to someone:

- 'I'm excited about the party tonight' or
- 'I am angry with you for not thanking me for doing that' or
- 'I think this TV programme stinks',

you are not hurting that person. You are letting her or him know about your feelings.

If someone tells you:
- 'I feel lonely' or
- 'I am sad my mum is ill' or
- 'I think I'd like to be your friend',

they are letting you know more about them. These are good ways of talking about feelings because they start by saying 'I am', 'I feel' and 'I think'.

If you say to someone:
- 'You are stupid',

you are talking about them in a bad way.

If you say instead:
- 'I think it was stupid of you to run across the road without looking',

you are letting them know how you feel about one thing in particular they did, not telling them that they are a stupid person. Of course, they may still not react well!

Being Responsible for Your Feelings

As I've said before, some people would like to be able to control other people's feelings and 'make' them feel a particular way about something. But this is just not possible. No one can 'make' you feel grateful or pleased or sad or angry or bored or anxious or whatever. Your feelings are not something that can be controlled by other people.

In fact, the only person who really knows and can think about your feelings is you.

As you know, the things we do are linked to the way we feel.

Tom is upset so he hides in his room.

Helen is angry with her brother so she slams the door.

But we also control the things we choose to do – Tom can choose to do something nice to try and make himself feel better; Helen can choose not to slam the door.

When Your Feelings Get You Down

If your feelings are getting you down, you can choose to think about them and see if you can change your response to them. You can turn things around and change them in this way because you are responsible for your feelings. (Of course, this doesn't mean that it is wrong to feel sad or angry or jealous or depressed – all these feelings are normal and everyone has them.)

James has been given a new bike. He is so excited that he immediately cycles round to his friend Tony's house to show him. When he gets there he finds Tony engrossed in a television show. James has to sit and wait for it to finish before Tony will come out and look at the new bike. James feels disappointed and hurt.

James can think about these feelings and he can choose:
- to think: 'If Tony were really my friend, he'd have turned off this stupid programme and come out at once to look at the bike'

or
- to think: 'This will soon be over. Just because Tony wants to see the end bit doesn't mean he doesn't want to see my bike'.

Mark would like to be in the school football team. He practises hard at weekends and does his best at the trials. He doesn't get chosen.

Mark can think about his feelings of disappointment and he can choose:
- to feel angry with the teacher for not choosing him and humiliated that all the effort he has made has not been recognised,

or
- to feel angry with himself and tell himself 'You're obviously hopeless',

or

- to tell himself, 'It's very disappointing not to get on the team, but I trained hard and did my best and no one can do more than that. That's OK'.

Amy's gran is ill and there is talk that she may have to go into hospital for an operation. Then Amy's friend Robert tells her that his grandmother has just died. Amy is very worried. She wonders if her gran is dying, but no one has told her the truth.

Amy can think about her feelings of fear and sadness. She can choose:

- to keep them to herself,

or

- to talk to her parents about them and find out the real situation. Perhaps Amy's gran is not dying. If she is dying, then it will help Amy and her parents if they can talk about it together and share their feelings.

(If someone you love has to go away or if that person is hurt or dies, you will feel full of pain and grief. If you want to cry, that's OK. Crying is a good thing to do – it's good to show your feelings.)

Being Responsible for Your Behaviour
We are all, adults and children, responsible for the way we behave.

This may seem an odd thing to say in a book addressed to children and young people who are constantly being told how to behave, what to do and what not to do, by all kinds of adults – parents, teachers, police officers, etc.

In fact, none of us – adults or children – can control every bit of our lives and make things happen the way we want them to, however hard we try:

Jackie auditions for the star part in the school play, but someone else is picked for it. She tried her hardest to get the part, but she can't make the drama teacher decide to give it to her.

Kenneth plans to hang out the washing, but then it starts to pour with rain. He can't control the weather, much as he'd like it to be a sunny day so that his best jeans will dry in time for an outing.

But even though Kenneth can't control the weather and Jackie can't control the drama teacher, they can control how they behave in these situations.

Jackie could feel depressed and upset and decide that she'll never try for a part in a play again. Alternatively, Jackie could decide to feel pleased that she had a go and tried her hardest even if it didn't work out; now she'll audition for one of the smaller parts.

Kenneth could feel fed up, but decide to make the best of it and look for another pair of trousers to wear. Alternatively, Kenneth could choose not to help himself and allow his feelings of upset to ruin his day completely; he could even refuse to go on the outing at all.

Of course, it's often very difficult to think through your feelings and find a way of helping yourself. Sometimes you may just feel overwhelmed.

CRYING IS A GOOD THING

Misusing the Idea of Being Responsible

Sometimes people misuse the idea of being responsible for their behaviour or they pretend that someone else 'made' them do something.

Thomas is taking his little sister Susan to the park while their mum is out. 'Mum said we could go on the swings or feed the ducks,' says Susan. 'I want to feed the ducks.'

'Mum said I'm in charge,' says Thomas, 'so I get to decide and I want to go on the swings.'

Thomas is using the idea of being in charge of looking after Susan as an excuse for getting his own way. Susan is too young to understand that he is being unfair.

Wendy and Nancy are playing a board game in Wendy's house. Nancy wins two games in a row and Wendy doesn't like being beaten. They start a third game and soon it's clear that Nancy will win this one too. Wendy suddenly tips up the board so all the pieces fall on the floor.

'Why did you spoil the game?' asks Nancy.

'You made me do it!' shouts Wendy. 'You kept on winning. It's your fault!'

65

Of course Nancy didn't 'make' Wendy spoil the game. Wendy chose to spoil the game all on her own – Wendy is entirely responsible for her own behaviour.

Michael's parents don't allow him to ride his bike in town as they think the traffic is too dangerous. Michael's friend Phyllis wants him to cycle into town with her. 'Your parents will never know,' she says. But Michael's mother catches sight of them as she drives through town and Michael gets into trouble when he gets home. 'You know you're not allowed to ride your bike in town,' says Mum, 'so why did you do it?'

'Phyllis made me go with her,' says Michael.

Sometimes someone persuades us to do something we're not sure about and we allow ourselves to be persuaded. Michael allowed himself to be persuaded by Phyllis, but Phyllis did not 'make' Michael ride his bike in town – Michael is responsible for his own behaviour.

Of course lots of adults are also confused about responsibility for their own behaviour:

When Mohan and Laxsmi's father arrives home from work, he finds them quarrelling and fighting over which TV programme to watch. Straight away, he tells

*their mother that he is going out again and he'll be
back later when things have calmed down. Their
mother is furious with them and shouts: 'You've made
your father, who is tired after a hard day at work, go
out again before he's eaten his dinner!'*

In fact, Mohan and Laxsmi's mother is wrong – the
children didn't 'make' their father leave. His decision to
leave was his responsibility. He could have chosen to
stay and asked the children to quieten down.

Whenever anyone (adults or other children) tells you
'You made me do that,' it's important to ask yourself
what your role was.

But if you genuinely didn't do anything wrong, say
to yourself, 'I didn't make that person do anything.

Other people are responsible for their own behaviour. I am only responsible for my behaviour.' This is an important way to stick up for yourself.

Of course, if a bully or a gang forces you to do something against your will or an adult misuses their authority to make you do something wrong or something that makes you feel uncomfortable, you are not responsible because you are in situation that you cannot control however much you want to. Try to look after yourself as best you can (run off if possible) and tell a trustworthy adult as soon as you can. See **Where to Get Help and Advice** at the end of this book.

DEVELOPING AND USING YOUR INNER POWER

You have power inside you that you may not even know about. You can learn to develop and use this inner power to stick up for yourself.

- If you learn to stick up for yourself, then other people can try to bully you, but the impact on you won't be so great.
- If you learn to stick up for yourself, you won't need to try to control other people by bullying and frightening them.

STICKING UP FOR YOURSELF

You may be thinking that it's a bit silly to tell you that you have power. After all, when you are a child you have to do what adults tell you to do. It's very clear that they have power over you.

Role Power
It's true that adults – parents and teachers, for example – have power over you. These people can tell you when to go to bed, what medicine to take, what to wear, decide how much pocket money you can have, when you may talk to your friends and so on. It can

seem as though you have no power at all.

The kind of power that these adults have over you is role power – the kind of power that is part of the job of being a parent or being a teacher.

There are lots of people in society with role power:

- the Prime Minister;
- nurses;
- traffic wardens;
- police officers;
- lifeguards;
- and so on.

These people have role power over other adults as well as over children; a police officer might tell you not to drop litter and tell an adult not to let their dog off the lead.

You may have some role power yourself – perhaps you're:

- captain of the swimming team
- head choir boy/girl
- a babysitter.

Janine is a babysitter for a two-year-old and a three-year-old. Her role as babysitter gives her the power to tell them that it's potty time or that they mustn't pull the cat's tail or stick their fingers into electric sockets.

The people with role power who manage that power best are those who give choices when it's possible:

Raymond is in charge of a Scout team which has organised a barbecue for the rest of the company on a camping trip. Now the clearing up has to be done. 'Shall we do it now or after the sing-song?' Raymond asks. 'Oh, let's get it over with!' the team decide.

Raymond has used his role power, but made his team feel powerful by giving them a choice.

Of course you don't have to like or agree with everything that people with role power over you make you do. It's sometimes possible to get them to change things – you might succeed, for example, in getting your parents to agree that you can now go to bed half an hour later. However, it's not very likely that you'd manage to persuade your teacher to never give homework for instance.

Some battles are worth fighting and some aren't – often it's not worth fighting people with role power over you, even if it's frustrating that they have that power.

Of course, this isn't true if that person is misusing their role power. If an adult with role power over you tries to get you to do something that feels uncomfortable or wrong, find an adult you trust, and tell her/him what happened.

You can still have inner power even though lots of people have role power over you.

Good Ways to Help Yourself Gain Inner Power

The power that you can have now and which depends entirely on you, is personal, inner power. If you spend your energy building up and using this inner power, you will be sticking up for yourself.

Here are some thoughts that might get in the way of the inner power that allows you to be glad to be you. It's all too easy to spend a lot of time worrying about them. Why not just let them go instead?

Letting Things Go

- Let go of the idea that to be liked you have to be like everyone else and fit in with what they want you to do. You don't have to think like them, wear the same clothes, listen to the same music – unless you want to. If you spend your time trying to be like others, there'll be no time left to be yourself.

- Let go of the idea that if someone doesn't like you, there must be something wrong with you (you might think you've said the wrong thing; you're not wearing the right clothes; you must be awful to be with). Stick up for yourself by starting to look at it this way: if someone doesn't like you, it's their problem not yours. Of course that doesn't mean that you shouldn't listen if someone tells you that something that you say or do upsets them. Other people have the right to stick up for themselves too!

- Let go of the idea that the people you like have to do what you are doing and like what you like all the time. Your friend can go and play football while you paint a picture and still be your friend; your friend can like different TV programmes from you and still be your friend; your friend can enjoy being with other friends and still be your friend. Allow your friends and the people you love to be different from you and to go off and do what's important to them.

- Let go of the idea that some people are always strong, tough and brave and able to cope and some people are always weak, soft and afraid and in need of help. In fact, we can all be strong and weak, afraid and tough. Sometimes it's nice to be strong and help other people and sometimes it's nice to cry and want to be looked after. You can have both.

- Let go of the idea that if your family really loved you, and if your friends were truly your friends, they would know what you want without you having to tell them. Remember that however well the people who care about you (your family, best friends and so on) know you, they are not mind-readers – they cannot know what you are thinking or hoping. Let them know. Tell them what you want and feel – otherwise you could be waiting around in vain for a long, long time.

- Let go of the idea that everyone has to like you. A bus conductor doesn't have to like you to give you a ticket; your dentist doesn't have to like you to fill a hole in your tooth.

- Let go of the idea that it's shameful to have needs and wants. It's not only not shameful, it's normal. Asking for what you want won't always get you what you want (such as a chance to try your friend's new bike; a trip to Disneyland; a party on your birthday; a hug from your dad), but not asking will only get you nowhere.

If you can let go of tormenting ideas such as these, you will begin to feel freer and stronger.

Allow Yourself to Be You!
Sometimes people are bullied because the bullies think they are 'different' in some way. The idea of people being different is something that frightens some people. But we are all different from each other. Each one of us, including you, is rare, individual, beautiful, special – in fact, absolutely unique. So, it's OK to be different. It's human to be different.

Part of being human and different is allowing yourself:
- to do what you want to do because you want to do it (so long as you are not hurting yourself or others).

As long as you don't hurt yourself or hurt anyone else or make them feel bad or break a family or school rule, or the law, doing what you want to do is OK. You don't always have to have a reason for everything or explain everything you do. If you feel like going for a walk in the rain so that you can feel the wetness on your face, then do it.

- to change your mind.

As you get older and become interested in new things and find out more about other things, you'll want to branch out in all kinds of ways. Allow yourself to change your mind – you can decide to be a brain surgeon rather than a pop star; you can change your favourite food from pizza to chips; you can change your favourite book from *The Tale of Peter Rabbit* to *The Lord of the Rings* and you can decide to like yourself instead of not liking yourself.

- to make mistakes.

There's no one in the world who doesn't make mistakes. When you're learning something new, you're sure to make lots of them – but don't give up, just keep trying! (Remember, if you got everything right the first time you tried it, your teachers would be out of a job.)

Sometimes you feel bad about making some kinds of mistakes – like forgetting to send a birthday card or breaking something or not doing something you promised to do. When this happens, the important thing is to try and mend the mistake (why not send that card, even if it's now a bit late). If that's not possible, apologise. Think of mistakes as a way of learning how to do things better (don't use them as excuses not to do things!).

One good way to build up your inner power is to remind yourself that you're great as you are. You don't have to:

- pretend to be something you're not;
- behave like someone else;
- dress like someone else.

Relax, and just be you!

Don't Lose Your Inner Power!

When you admire someone, you care very much about what they think of you. You tend to look up to them and perhaps behave in a way that you think will please them. You might even copy the way they behave. This is not necessarily all bad – we can learn a lot by observing people we admire and seeing if the way that they do things works for us.

But in this kind of situation, it's easy to lose some of our inner power to that person or those people we admire. It's important, too, not to get too starry-eyed

DON'T PICK ON ME

about people you admire. At first it may seem as if they have all the answers, but in fact, the only person who really knows what is best for you, is you. Of course, there's a difference between idolising others (imagining they know better than us) and listening to the views of those who may really be better informed or helpful to us.

Mark thinks Peter and Robert are great and he'd really like to be their friend. Mark gets his mum to buy him the kind of sweatshirt and trainers that Peter and Robert have and he starts going to computer club after school because they go. When he finds out they like skateboarding, he starts getting into this too.

Perhaps Mark will make friends with Peter and Robert. Perhaps then he'll relax and do things because they please him, not because he wants to please other people. Of course, he may find that he really does like the same things as Peter and Robert! We often learn about what we like by being introduced to new things by other people.

Joanna has a riding lesson every weekend at a local stables. One day, Belinda, who owns her own horse and is a very good rider, starts chatting to her. 'You

*can have a ride on my horse next week if you want
to,' she says. Joanna is so excited and grateful that
Belinda has been friendly that she feels she has to stay
late and help her muck out.*

This may be the start of a good friendship and it may
not. Perhaps Belinda is a kind, friendly person who will
find it fun to help Joanna learn more about riding. But
what if she isn't? What if Joanna turns up next week
and Belinda is impatient and sneers at the way Joanna
rides?

How do you judge whether things are going well or
badly for you when you are with someone you admire?
Even if the person you admire is older than you or
better than you at doing something, in a good
friendship each person respects the other.

How can you tell if this is so?

Listen to your feelings – they will tell you. If you feel:

- comfortable;
- relaxed;
- respected as a person;
- welcome for just being you or
- like you're enjoying yourself,

then good. It's right for you.

If you feel:
- uneasy;
- anxious;
- uncomfortable;
- put-down or
- scared

then something is not right. What is it that is making you anxious? Are you worried you are not good enough? Is it something to do with the way you are being treated? If you go on feeling like this when you are with this person then perhaps it is not right for you. Don't stay in situations or go on seeing people who make you feel bad.

Sometimes you'll find that you get along fine with someone most of the time – but then they do something which leaves you feeling powerless and as though there is something wrong with you.

Juliet and Liz like to go to the shopping centre in town on Saturdays to look round and to have a Coke. But one day Juliet doesn't turn up at the bus stop to meet Liz as agreed. Liz waits and waits and then goes round to Juliet's house to find her. 'Oh, I can't make it today,' Juliet says casually, 'You don't mind, do you?' Liz does mind. She feels angry and humiliated. She wonders if Juliet didn't come because she doesn't really like her.

This is a horrible feeling for Liz to have. She has to put up with the disappointment of Juliet not turning up and then the worry that it might be because there's something wrong with her. What can she do to get rid of this awful, bullying feeling?

Liz is losing her power in this relationship to Juliet. That's why she's feeling so powerless. Liz can't make Juliet turn up at the bus stop, but there are steps she can take. She can:

- be realistic about how reliable Juliet is. Liz may still want to have Juliet as a friend, but she can take care not to put herself in a situation where she is reliant on Juliet to turn up.
- tell Juliet how inconsiderate she has been.
- in future arrange to call for Juliet at her house instead of hanging about at the bus stop. If she still wants to see her, that is.
- in future invite someone else to go to the shopping centre with her instead of or as well as Juliet.
- think to herself: 'Juliet is a fool to miss out on an afternoon with me. Her loss!'

If Liz does these things she will take back the power she lost to Juliet. In the future, if people let her down, Liz can say to herself: 'When people don't stick to arrangements, it's usually because something unexpected has happened, like an accident. If it's because they couldn't be bothered, more fool them to miss out on being with me.' By doing this, Liz will be slamming the door shut on any bullying feelings she has in herself and making herself less vulnerable to getting hurt by Juliet and people like her.

Inner Power Forever

Now you know a lot about inner power and you can begin to build up your inner power and use it. When you have inner power, you are in charge of yourself.

You can stick up for yourself because you know that:

- no one can 'make' you feel something (whether it's glad or sad). You and you alone are responsible for your feelings.
- no one can 'make' you do things you shouldn't do (as in 'you made me do it'). You and you alone are responsible for your behaviour and others are responsible for theirs.
- you can choose to feel good about yourself even when things don't go right.
- you can learn to make choices that are good for you.
- you can recognise your feelings. You know that it's good to have all of them (the angry, shy, ashamed and frightened ones as well as the excited, glad, joyous ones) because that's what makes you a complete person.

- your needs are important. You know what they are and you can try to get them met.

By holding on to your inner power you can choose not to be powerless in your relationships with people. You can begin to make friends with people with whom you have equal power and avoid situations that make you feel powerless.

PART THREE

Helping Yourself to Feel Good

HAPPINESS WORKOUTS

Be a good friend to yourself by practising these exercises. They will help to remind you of all the good things about you and this in turn will help you to stick up for yourself.

Happiness Workout No.1: When You Feel Lonely or Sad

When you feel lonely or sad, give yourself a treat – do something nice for yourself that you enjoy. It doesn't have to be something that costs money or something very complicated to organise. You could:

- stroke a friendly cat;

- have a long, hot bath;
- watch a sunset;
- look in your favourite shop window;
- draw a picture;
- watch your favourite comedy show on TV;
- call someone you like and feel comfortable talking to;
- listen to your favourite music.

Start a list of things like these that you enjoy. When you enjoy something new, add it to your list so that it's not forgotten. And don't just keep these nice things for when you're feeling lonely or sad – look at your list from time to time and if you enjoyed, say, going to the park and watching the ducks swimming about, find time to do it again.

Happiness Workout No.2: Nice Things About You
Being a good friend to yourself means that you can say nice things to yourself about you. You can also remind yourself of all the things that you can do.

Make two lists: one of nice things about you and one of the things that you can do. You can include things like 'I'm a good swimmer' even if you're not the best swimmer in your school (you don't have to be a champion at things to be able to include them). These are your personal lists and your personal good things about you, so don't hold back!

You might include things like:

Nice Things I Know About Me

- I'm a good friend to have.
- I like animals.
- I have beautiful eyelashes.
- I'm a good listener.

Things I Can Do

- I'm good at catching.
- I know a lot about astronomy.
- I'm a good speller.
- I've got a good memory.
- I'm good at art.

When something happens that makes you think 'Why would anyone like me anyway?' or 'I messed that up. I can't get anything right,' remember all the things listed under 'Nice Things I Know About Me' and 'Things I Can Do' and be kinder to yourself. The nice things that you have listed will help you to stick up for yourself inside and be less critical.

Happiness Workout No.3: Look After Yourself

Get into the habit of doing something good for your body and something good for your brain every day. It could be:

Body
- Getting exercise (going swimming or going for a walk);
- Eating some fruit;
- Washing your hair;
- Cutting your toenails.

Brain
- Following a story on the news;
- Solving a puzzle;
- Learning a song;
- Browsing in the library;
- Reading a book;
- Drawing a picture.

If you can do things like these, you are finding good ways to look after yourself.

Happiness Workout No.4: The Letting Go Technique

Is your stomach tight? Are your fists clenched? Are your nails bitten? Does your chest feel empty and hurting? Do you have a headache? Are your teeth clenched? Are your shoulders tight and high instead of loose and relaxed?

When your body feels clenched and tight in ways like this, it is showing you that you are anxious or frightened or sad or hurting. Listen to what your body is telling you and look after these feelings.

Your body talks to you all the time and lets you know when things are going well for you and when they're not. Keep in touch with your body and listen to its messages. Look after your body by letting the tightness or emptiness or pain go out of it.

Memorise or ask a friend to read these directions to you slowly. They should pause after each one and give you plenty of time to do what is asked.

1. Lie down on the floor with your eyes closed.
2. Tuck your chin in slightly so that your spine and neck feel long and comfortable.
3. Feel the floor holding up your body.
4. Take a deep breath right down into your tummy. Let it out slowly.
5. Take another deep breath right down into your

tummy. Let it out slowly.

6. Imagine lying in warm sand at the seaside. Imagine each part of your body leaving its shape in the sand.

7. Slowly relax each bit of you into the sand starting with your head and working down to your toes. Let all the tightness run out of you.

8. Lie quietly for a few moments breathing deeply.

9. When you're ready, sit up slowly and open your eyes.

Happiness Workout No.5: The Praise Box

Whenever someone says something nice to you about you or praises something you have done, write it down in a special notebook or on bits of paper that you can store away in a praise box. Open your praise box or notebook every so often and remind yourself of all the nice things that have been said by all these different people.

Happiness Workout No.6: The Difference Game

Play this game with a friend or someone in your family. Sit down together and take it in turns to:

- Tell each other all the things that make you different from each other.
- Tell each other all the things you like about each other.

This game will help to remind you how different, unique and special each person is – including you!

Happiness Workout No.7: Writing Affirmations

An affirmation is a way of letting yourself or someone else know how much you value the good things about yourself or them.

You and your friends could get together in a group, each with your own blank notebook. The idea is that you pass each notebook around the group and everybody writes in the positive things they have learned about each person in their notebook (what their strengths are, nice things about them and so on).

Each group member can then keep their notebook. That way, if you ever feel down, you can turn to the notebook and remind yourself of other people's positive opinions about you.

PART FOUR

Protecting Yourself

In Part Two of this book we looked at making changes in the way you feel about yourself so that, if you are being bullied, you won't feel so unsafe inside and, if you are a bully, so that you won't need to hurt other people in order to feel better about yourself.

In this section there are some practical things that people who are being bullied, whether at school or at home, can do to protect themselves. I also suggest things that people who bully can do to help themselves to stop behaving in such a bullying way. If you are someone who witnesses bullying taking place, it can be very disturbing – there are ideas for things that you can do in that situation at the end of this section.

GENERAL ADVICE FOR PEOPLE WHO ARE BEING BULLIED

Here are some ideas for people who are being bullied:

- Stick with your friends whenever you can. Try to be part of a group.
- If you don't have friends, or they are not around, try to keep within sight of a teacher or supervisor.
- Try not to react to teasing or bullying by showing that you are upset or angry. Try to keep and look calm. Bullies can lose interest in people who don't react.
- Don't make a show of wearing expensive jewellery or taking other expensive items into school with you.

DON'T SHOW OFF BY WEARING EXPENSIVE JEWELLERY OR TAKING OTHER EXPENSIVE ITEMS INTO SCHOOL...

- Be aware of your behaviour – do other people seem to get irritated with you when you just want them to notice and like you, for example? Why not observe how people you admire make friends or get to join in with others.

- If bullies take your lunch money or steal something of yours, try not to get into a fight. It's not worth being beaten up for the price of a school lunch. Tell a trusted adult what happened and who was responsible as soon as you can and talk through how you're going to ensure that it doesn't happen again.

- Practise your replies to things that you may be teased or bullied about (embarrassing initials, unusual name, spectacles, hearing aid, red hair, freckles, tall, short, plump, etc.) so that you can give the impression that it doesn't bother you.

- If you receive an abusive or threatening text, email or chatroom message, do not reply. If you do, you will encourage the bully.

- If a bully accuses you of saying or doing something bad to them, you could try saying something like, 'I'm sorry if I said/did something that hurt your feelings. I didn't mean to.' This acknowledges the bully's feelings and may help to calm them down.

- Stand up to a bully. To try this, you have to choose your moment – preferably wait for when the bully's friends are not there to see what's going on. If there are other people around, the bully may feel that they can't be seen to back down. Try to look confident and relaxed and say something direct like, 'You may not like me, but I want you to know that I'm not going to care what you say/let you bully me/hurt me/take my things any more!' Of course this may not work – and don't ever put yourself at risk if you think it won't – but if you sense that it might, it's worth a try. Bullies expect the people they bully to be afraid, so if you surprise them by standing up to them, they might just back down.

- Talk your way out. If you're good at using words or good at verbal arguments, this is worth a try. If you've got a sense of humour too, you might even be able to joke your way out of a tight spot. But take care! Don't let the bullies think that you're laughing at them or that you think they are stupid. You'd be surprised how many professional comedians began telling jokes as a way of avoiding being bullied at school.

- Threaten to tell and say: 'I have a right to protect myself!' Bullies have no right to hurt you. Go for it! But be sure you follow up and do tell. You might think that telling an adult or someone older about

DON'T PICK ON ME

bullying is cowardly. This is not so. If someone is trying to hurt you, you have the right to get someone older or someone in authority like your teacher to protect you. Protecting children and young people is part of the job for teachers, playground supervisors and police officers as it is for parents. Not all of them, unfortunately, can be relied on to stop bullying in a gentle, wise and tactful way, but when you risk being beaten up, the important thing is to stop the violence quickly before you get hurt. Your action may also help protect others who are being bullied.

Just because you are being bullied now does not mean that this horrible situation will go on forever. It is possible, especially with the right kind of help and support, for life to get better. There are plenty of examples of adults (have a look in Part One) who were bullied when they were children who went on to have happy and successful lives.

Teasing

As I said earlier, teasing is different from verbal bullying. Teasing is essentially good-humoured and you can feel free to tease back. Lots of people at school get teased. This can be hard to take if you're not used to it. People who have been teased a lot at home by sisters and brothers find it easier to cope with because they have had a lot of experience. Try to keep a sense of humour if you can!

If you're finding teasing upsetting, it's a good idea to prepare yourself for it.

If you've got to have braces on your teeth, for example, and tomorrow is the first time you'll appear at school with them, why not think about how you might be teased about them and what you can say in reply:

- I've been signed up to star in the next *Jaws* movie.
- You have to suffer to be beautiful.

Ask your mum or dad or some other caring person to help you prepare for possible teasing. They might have ideas on what you can say, or pretend to be the teaser and you can try out your replies. This will help to give you confidence. (You might even find, to your surprise, that no one comments on your braces the next day at school.)

The other thing to remember about teasing is that if you choose not to react, you probably won't get teased. Teasers like the people they tease to react and if you don't react, they will probably stop.

Trying to Avoid a Fight

Perhaps you know the Bible story about David and Goliath? David the shepherd boy goes out to fight the champion of the Philistines, a huge man called Goliath who is armed with a shield and a spear and covered with armour. Tiny David has nothing, but his shepherd's staff, a sling and five pebbles and yet he succeeds in killing Goliath. (Of course, he has God on his side too . . .)

There are lots of stories like this about the small and weak defeating the big and powerful in a fight. Unfortunately, in almost all fights in playgrounds and elsewhere, it is the small, the weak and those who aren't good fighters, or who don't want to fight, who get pulverised by the big, powerful bullies.

The most sensible thing you can do when faced with a bully who is threatening you physically is to follow the advice of the old saying:

Run, run, run away,
Live to fight another day.

(Hopefully, you'll find a way so that you don't have to fight 'another day' either. Who needs the hassle?)

If you can't walk away or avoid the bullies who want to fight you or beat you up, some of these tactics may be useful:

- Try to bluff your way out – for example, you could

pretend that a teacher is waiting for you or that your dad is on his way to pick you up.

- Walk away if you can. A fight takes two people – if you refuse to fight, this can stop the bully from hurting you. This can be a hard thing to do because it can appear that the bully has won – perhaps it might appear that you have accepted the bully's insults. If your friends are watching, you might feel honour-bound to stand there and try to fight in case they think you are a coward. But remember, if you manage to walk away without a fight taking place, you will have succeeded in leaving without you being physically hurt and without resorting to violence and possibly hurting someone else. It takes great strength and courage to turn your back on the jeers and taunts and walk away.

- Lots of fights start with a person who decides that they have been insulted:

  'What did you call me?'

  'Who do you think you're staring at?'

  'Say that again, if you dare!'

Bullies who enjoy fights like to seek out reasons to feel insulted on purpose – it gives them an excuse to beat someone up!

This kind of fight often happens in playgrounds and everyone rushes to watch. Because there is an audience, a bully is not likely to back down easily. In an ideal world, a good friend of the person who is being picked on would run off to find a teacher to stop the fight developing. (But this isn't always an ideal world and people are sometimes scared of being called a tell-tale.)

- If you find yourself being picked on by a bully who is trying to start a fight, try to keep thinking and stay cool even if you are being insulted. Try not to be drawn into insulting the bully back. If you can, agree with the bully. For example, if the bully calls you 'four-eyes' because you wear glasses and accuses you of being afraid to fight, you can agree that, yes, you do wear glasses and, yes, you don't like to fight. Agreeing to things like these doesn't mean you are a coward – they are facts and nothing to be ashamed of.

- If the bully insults you in abusive ways or says horrible things that aren't true, disagree, but try to do it in a calm way. You could simply say, for example, 'That is not true.' Don't throw insults back.

- What bullies always want is to get a reaction from the people they bully – they want you to get angry or to look scared. If you can manage not to react to the insults you might manage to get away without being beaten up or having to fight. Keep walking and looking straight ahead.

Should You Learn to Fight?

Even if you become a karate black belt, there is no guarantee that you will never be bullied ever again. However, being taught to fight properly will give you confidence and may reduce your chances of being bullied. Just the fact that you look more confident may lessen your chances of being picked on.

The best way to learn to fight is to join a self-defence class or a class that teaches one of the martial arts such as karate. Your local library should be able to help you find out what's available in your area.

Classes like these can be a big help in making you feel more confident when you are faced with aggression. They will help you protect yourself and deal with the aggression without being frightened. They should also teach you ways of getting out of threatening situations by non-violent means. It's good to know you can defend yourself, but better not to use it if you don't need to.

If you are someone who fights in order to get your own way and to bully and control other people, you could also find these classes useful as they will teach you how to use your anger and aggression and fighting skills in more positive ways.

But it is very important to be realistic about what you can achieve by learning self-defence or one of the martial arts. Remember that:

- You will not turn into Wonder Woman or Superman, so you must not start taking silly risks.
- Self-defence and martial arts techniques need to be practised and kept up or your skills will rust. Even with training you could be overpowered.
- Fighting back physically is just one possible way to handle a situation in which you are being threatened and should be a last resort to keep you safe. Don't forget to try the other, non-violent options first.

Homophobic Bullying

It can be hard enough to tell an adult about ordinary bullying, but some young gay people, or people who think they might be gay, find it too difficult to report being called abusive names just at the point in their lives when they are feeling self-conscious about their sexual identity and may wish to keep things private. If this is happening to you, you may find some of the helplines listed at the back of this book useful.

Don't give up on your school though. There are some good examples of ways that schools have helped to support young gay people. In one Lancashire school, for example, teachers became aware of anti-gay name-calling and began to crack down on it. They also started a project to tackle the problem in other ways. One fifteen-year-old pupil said: 'If my brother was annoying me I would say, "You're gay". I didn't really know anyone who was gay and I hadn't realised it might offend or upset some people. Since the project I have tried to use it less and most other people have too.' Another pupil said, 'While we were doing the project one of my friends told me she was bisexual which I don't know if she would have done otherwise. It has made everyone much more able to talk about it sensibly.'

Blackmail

Sometimes bullies will try to make you do something or give them something by threatening to tell the world a secret they know about you that you would like kept private. This is called blackmail. The best way to deal with blackmail, if at all possible, is to say, 'Tell whoever you like. I don't care!' This takes a lot of courage. (We all have embarrassing secrets.) If you can, talk to a trusted adult about the problem – your secret may not be as embarrassing as you think.

Text and Online Bullying

Texting, social networking sites and chatrooms have become part of most people's lives and are usually a useful and enjoyable way to keep in touch with friends and family.

But remember that real friendship involves being

with people in the real world, interacting with them and spending time together. It is important not to become reliant on cyber-relationships to the exclusion of interaction with real people in the real world. Real relationships can sometimes be difficult (even best friends sometimes fall out!) but they usually allow opportunities for misunderstandings or bad times to be talked about and sorted out.

Some young people show off about the number of friends they have online and boast about how popular they are. But are all these online 'friends' real friends? If they include people you have only met online, these friendships are not real. Indeed there is no way of knowing whether these online 'friends' are who they say they are or whether they mean what they say. A fantasy world can easily be created into which you can find yourself drawn.

Perhaps you feel lonely and are having a hard time making friends in the real world. Perhaps you are feeling misunderstood by your family and are angry and resentful. In situations such as these it can be tempting to idealise someone you chat to online and imagine that they really understand you. This can tempt you to open up to them and trust them with information about yourself that in the real world you would probably only divulge to a close friend you know to be reliable. In this way, some young people can make themselves vulnerable to cyber-'friends' who turn out not to be reliable or trustworthy; some even turn out to be malicious bullies who use the internet to glean information about people that they then use against them.

Developments in communications technology have unfortunately provided bullies with lots of new ways to bully. These include:

- sending threatening or insulting messages.
- posting private or personal things about you so that you feel exposed and vulnerable. This can even include posting embarrassing photographs you didn't know someone had taken.
- adding spiteful and malicious comments of a personal kind to discussions on a forum or website which can then encourage others (who may not even know you) to join in with the abuse. This is called 'flaming'.
- using the internet to deliberately start problems, insult, hurt or antagonise you for their own amusement. This is called trolling. The troll's aim is to wind you up to the point where you respond indignantly or seriously to whatever nonsense they have posted.
- using your name and details to set up a social

network page without your knowledge or consent. This is called 'identity theft'. The bully can then leave false opinions and comments that make you appear to be a silly or nasty person.

- pretending that you think horrible things about individuals or groups and posting those claims on websites or in chatrooms together with your personal details so that you receive angry or abusive messages.

If this has happened to you, it can be very distressing. The cyber-world that is created online feels 'real' and as though it exists everywhere – even in our own homes. Perhaps that is why cyber-bullying can feel so intrusive – as though there is nowhere you are safe from the bullies. It can also make you feel very isolated. Try to remember that these horrible comments about you or mean messages are actually nothing to do with you as you really are. Of course, it can be hard to hold on to your knowledge of yourself as an OK person in situations like these.

Tell an adult what is happening if you feel able to. You need help from your parents or school to deal with this. Government guidance to schools on bullying officially acknowledges the problem of cyber-bullying, so your school should be aware of this problem.

If you are receiving abusive texts, you or a trusted adult can report the bully's phone number to your mobile phone company's nuisance call hotline. New technology is also being developed to block messages from certain numbers. If you are being abused on forums or in chatrooms, the bullies can be tracked down. Many cyber-bullies don't realise that they can now be investigated and caught by service providers, by IT technicians and by the police.

Here are some other things you can do to help yourself.

- However tempting, never reply to abusive texts, emails or chatroom messages. If you do, you will encourage the bully.
- Let a trusted adult know what is happening so you feel supported.
- Keep abusive messages or pictures. They can be used as evidence should you decide to report the matter to your school or to the police.
- Only post information about yourself in a forum or chatroom that you are happy for everyone to know.
- Don't post personal details about yourself (address, phone number, where you go to school, your plans for the weekend, where you'll be, etc) on an open forum.
- Don't reply to missed calls unless you know the

number. If it's a genuine caller, they will call back.

- Only give your mobile number, email or chatroom address to family and close friends. Ask friends not to pass on these details and take care not to pass on their details. Help each other to have good cyber-habits and keep safe.
- If you play games online, use a nickname and don't choose one that could attract the wrong kind of attention.
- Don't believe everything that is said online. Take it with a big pinch of salt.
- Ask your parents or school to help you with security settings so that only your real friends have access to information about you on social networking sites.

You may find it helps to chat online to other pupils who have been bullied – www.pupiline.net was set up by a boy who was himself bullied with the aim of giving similarly victimised pupils the chance to talk to each other.

Group Bullying

It's easy for a group of bullies to make even the most confident person feel isolated, friendless, weak, lonely and powerless; you may even begin to wonder if there isn't, after all, something wrong with you. (Answer: No!) This can be the hardest kind of bullying to deal with, especially if it goes on for any length of time. If this is happening to you, don't try to cope with it on your own – no one could. Try to find a trustworthy person to tell, perhaps your parent or a teacher, or a friend.

Some bullies seek out situations where they can have an audience because they enjoy being surrounded by admirers and supporters and having their every word listened to intently. If they use sarcasm or wit to bully the victim and/or some physical violence, they like an appreciative crowd. In this situation, the level of cruelty and violence used by the bully or bullies to torment the victim can increase just because there is an audience to play up to.

In this gang or group situation, those taking part in these cruel and hurtful activities may not feel personal responsibility. This is because so many others are also taking part and 'sharing' the blame. In fact, even though they are not acting alone, each and every one of the bullies taking part in group bullying is personally responsible for what takes place.

Many children who are part of a group of bullies would not behave in this way if they were on their own. If this is happening to you, you should be aware that the desire to be part of a group or gang can sometimes lead you into saying or doing cruel and evil things that you would not dream of saying or doing if you were on your own.

Being different to everyone else in the gang or refusing to do something everyone else is doing can be difficult and painful and make you afraid that you will lose your friends. Sometimes a group or gang will use jeers and threats to make you go along with what they want to do ('You're chicken!' 'Why not run home to Mummy?').

When you go along with something that you wouldn't do as an individual, you are avoiding taking responsibility for your actions. You pretend to yourself that what is happening isn't your fault, you didn't start it.

The fact is, however, that your very presence may be encouraging the bully or bullies by giving them an audience.

These group/gang situations are hard to handle, but it is always possible that if you are uncomfortable or shocked about something the group/gang is doing then some of the others may be too – perhaps they are also too scared to say so. You could try appealing to the nicer people to support you in not taking part or stopping what is being done. If the situation is really out of hand you should not take part, saying why if you can. You should also try to leave or call for help.

You need to be aware of the dangers of the group/gang way of thinking so that you can recognise it and avoid becoming a victim of it. As a member of a group or gang you must also be able to avoid being pressurised into going along with something that you will later regret and feel ashamed about.

WHO STARTED IT?

Sometimes someone who is being bullied fights back or perhaps even attacks first, either physically or verbally, in a desperate attempt to stop the bully hurting them again. If a teacher or some other adult who does not know anything about the bullying that has been going on, spots this, they might misinterpret the situation and blame the victim for bullying instead of the real bully. Some bullies are very good at behaving well in front of adults or lying so these adults may find it difficult to believe you when you say you have been bullied.

If this happens to you, it is very hard. Try to get your friends or other witnesses to come with you and explain what really happened. Your parents may also be able to help you sort things out.

Of course, we hope that teachers and other adults will take care when they investigate incidents of bullying to ensure that they are getting the whole story.

They should not assume that what they happened to see was an isolated incident. In fact, it might be just one example among very many of bullying taking place. You might find it helps to keep a diary in which you write down what happened and when and whether anyone else saw what was happening.

A school with an effective anti-bullying policy should be aware of this problem and have a way of investigating incidents of bullying thoroughly.

TURNING TO ADULTS FOR HELP

When bullying occurs, adult help is almost always needed to deal with it, and that adult help can be effective if properly carried out.

When Maxine's teacher found out that she was being bullied she had a quiet word with the bullies and then kept an eye on them. She also made sure that Maxine had opportunities to join in more and make friends.

These days many more adults, particularly teachers, are aware of bullying and the need to handle it sensitively and tactfully. Your school may also have a school counsellor to whom you could talk in confidence. Many police forces take bullying seriously these days, especially when there are issues of assault and harassment or racial, homophobic and cyber-bullying.

Your parents and teachers may find the end section of this book which lists organisations involved with bullying helpful – many offer advice and information on strategies to deal with bullying.

Unfortunately, some adults do not always deal with things well when told about bullying:

When Janine told her mum about being taunted and pushed around on the playground her mum told her it would soon stop. If it was still going on next term she would do something about it.

When Theresa's head teacher talked in assembly about bullying, she did it in such a way that it was obvious to the bullies that Theresa had 'told' on them. From then on, Theresa was bullied worse than before.

When Andrew told his dad about the boys who threw his sports kit around the changing room and tore his shirt, his dad went straight round to the school the next day and threatened to punch the bullies. Andrew was jeered at and taunted for the rest of the term.

It can make you feel quite despairing to have finally

plucked up the courage to tell an adult about being bullied, only to find that they will not help or that they have made the situation worse. You need to find another adult who may find it easier to understand and sort out. You could also try the helplines listed at the end of this book where you can talk in confidence to a sympathetic adult who has been trained to help young people in your situation. In a study done by one bullying helpline, it was found that nearly three quarters of the children who had used the service found that it had positive effects.

Telling About Bullying

The rule that you should never tell about bullying is a rule invented by bullies for their own benefit. Obviously, it makes things very convenient for them. Not only can they bully without getting caught, but a victim of their bullying cannot complain about it without being called a 'grass', a 'tell-tale', a 'cry-baby' or a 'wimp'.

Some adults are confused about whether telling about bullying is a good thing or a bad thing. Many of them were taught as children that bullying is 'good for you' (it 'builds character', it 'toughens you up'), or that it's something you learn to cope with as you get older, or that there's something dishonourable or humiliating in asking for help when you're being bullied – that you ought to be able to deal with it yourself. This idea (that bullying is something you should be able to cope with on your own) is very widespread. It's also totally untrue. The people who work on telephone helplines report fewer calls from older children even though people in this age group are still bullied – perhaps they are embarrassed to ask for help, feeling that they should be able to cope on their own.

Some people do find ways to cope on their own, but some can't. Sometimes the bullying is so severe that no one could deal with it on their own. Remember, even adults are bullied! There is never anything wrong with asking for help; in fact, it takes great courage and strength to do it.

Good Ways to Tell

- Remember that not telling helps the bullies go on bullying – and you are almost certainly not the only person who is or will be bullied by them. By telling you will be helping to create an atmosphere where people can feel safe and confident that they will be well treated instead of feeling frightened and insecure because they might be bullied.

- Keep a bullying diary. Note down what happens and when and if there were any witnesses. If you have been sent abusive texts or emails keep them as evidence.

- Tell someone if you can and take a friend or a witness or your mum or dad with you. It's good to have someone there for you.
- Don't suffer bullying for a long time. Perhaps you want to try and stop it on your own. That's fine. But if you don't manage to, don't let it drag on. Get help. The longer bullying goes on, the harder it will be to put an end to it and the more hurt you will be.

- As a last resort, and if your school really won't help the bullying to stop, it may be possible for you to change schools. Discuss this with your parents.

Adults Who Allow Bullying

Of course, you need to find the right kind of adult to help, and sometimes this isn't easy. Unfortunately bullying can be encouraged if some adults seem secretly to approve of such behaviour. If children discover that bullying others or 'throwing their weight around' gets them what they want and adults turn a blind eye to this kind of behaviour or even applaud it, bullying behaviour will go on as both bullies and their victims will come to believe that bullying must be acceptable.

Sometimes run-down areas may have an atmosphere of violence or a high crime rate, and people can grow up thinking that aggressive behaviour pays off and people cannot rely on outside help. Bullying behaviour may also be encouraged by their parents and their neighbours who think being a good fighter, having 'street cred' or being the toughest kid on the block is a good thing.

Even with an anti-bullying policy in their school some teachers may still believe that bullying is a 'normal' part of life's 'hard knocks' and the only way for children to learn to cope with bullying is to be 'toughened up' by experiencing it. This attitude can be found in public schools, where bullies might come from highly privileged backgrounds, to state schools, with children from run-down neighbourhoods. Fortunately, not all teachers are like this.

How Adults Should Deal With Bullying

If you tell an adult about being bullied you don't want them to act hastily and possibly make things worse for you. Try suggesting that they talk the situation through with you first. If you are being bullied, you usually want the adult you tell to do three things:

1. Stop the bullying.
2. Stop the bullying in such a way that neither the bully nor anyone else knows that you have told. (Sometimes this is not possible.)
3. Treat the bully firmly, but with understanding. Often you will be afraid that if the bully suffers because you have told, it will rebound on you.

Sometimes even the most sensible, sensitive and experienced adult is not able to manage all three things. Sometimes it's inevitable that a bully gets to know that you have told. (In this case, the adult should work out in advance how to handle things so you won't be tormented even more or isolated by your classmates.) If you tell your mum or dad, they will have to work out with the school how best to proceed.

A School Anti-bullying Policy

Since 2006, all UK schools have been required to have an anti-bullying policy. The government wants schools to have a 'zero tolerance' approach to bullying and all head teachers are urged to sign an anti-bullying 'Charter for Action' which sets out a series of actions for teachers to take. Concern has been expressed that some head teachers are still not taking the problem seriously enough and an Anti-Bullying Alliance was recently launched by the government to train teachers and pupils in the best ways of stopping bullying and resolving disputes.

These days, the courts take the view that schools have a duty to protect children from bullying. Some parents have even tried taking their child's school to court for not preventing bullying from taking place. A High Court judge recently defined bullying as 'conduct which intentionally caused hurt, either physical or psychological, which was unprovoked and which persisted over time'. This means that the bully or bullies hurt you, either physically or psychologically; that they did it on purpose; that you did nothing to cause them to behave in this way; and that the bullying went on for some time. The parents (or the young person) would have to be able to prove that there had been a pattern of bullying and that it had gone on for some time. The Human Rights Act also

119

requires that people should not be badly treated.

To really tackle the problem of bullying, it is important for your school not just to deal with it each time it occurs, but to have an anti-bullying charter, an agreed statement setting out students' rights not to be bullied and the actions that should be taken to ensure this. Children and young people can play an important part in putting such a policy together because it must be tailor-made for their particular school.

These days school anti-bullying policies help create an atmosphere in which pupils feel safe and confident that if bullying does occur, it will be noticed and dealt with both wisely and speedily.

Of course, schools cannot guarantee that bullying will never again take place. No school can realistically wipe out bullying overnight. It's important that every school constantly monitors how well their policy is working to keep the school bully-free.

Here are some ideas that your teachers might find useful in writing the anti-bullying policy for your school:

- The whole school should be organised in such a way that no one teacher or pupil is left to cope with a bullying problem alone. Everyone who works or studies at the school – the head, the teachers, the caretaker, the dinner ladies, the playground supervisors, the pupils, the governors, and so on – should all be involved in monitoring and tackling bullying.

- Everyone should be made aware that bullying is not allowed in the school in any form. A statement to this effect should be drawn up and given to every pupil and their parents. The statement should also emphasise the positive role that everyone can play in encouraging caring and responsible attitudes to other people.

- Teachers need to be well trained in how to handle incidents of bullying. Some intervene too quickly and make the problem worse. John, who was bullied at his grammar school, said, 'Teachers are too quick to dismiss bullying as horseplay and tell children to shake hands. But that only makes the problem worse because the bully thinks he has got away with it and can bully the other child even more for snitching on him.'

- Incidences of cyber-bullying should be referred to the school's IT expert so that the bullies can be tracked down. Acceptable ways to use cyber-communications should be established and made part of the school's anti-bullying policy.

- Pupils and teachers should discuss the layout of the school and its grounds and the routes taken by

pupils to and from school. They should identify where bullying takes place (for example, the corridors, classrooms when it's wet playtime, the toilets, the school bus) and at what time of day. Proper supervision of these areas should then be organised.

- Pupils and teachers should discuss which groups of people are more likely to be bullied (for example, new first years, ethnic minority pupils, people who transfer from other schools, people who are placed in special classes and so on) and see whether there are ways they can be helped to feel safe. It might be possible, for example, for older pupils to be given the responsibility of looking after new first years as they settle in – showing them around, taking a friendly interest, being alert to any anxieties or threats of bullying. Some schools ask older pupils to act as 'buddies' or mentors to new pupils.

- When children from ethnic minorities suffer racial bullying they may feel unable to approach their teacher for help if the teacher does not come from a similar background. Ethnic minority communities who have experience of providing support and techniques for surviving the harshness of racism may have much advice to offer schools in such cases.

- Large secondary schools can be very frightening places for new pupils. Older pupils could help by preparing maps, notices and signs for them so that they can easily find their way around.

- Pupils and teachers could organise regular discussions of bullying and issues connected with bullying. This might include studying particular books, plays or programmes which examine the issues (see suggestions at the end of this book).

- Pupils who carry weapons should be excluded from school.

IF YOU'VE BEEN BULLIED

If you've experienced being bullied and threatened, you'll need to tell someone you trust what happened and talk it through. Situations of this kind are very frightening. You might also be feeling angry or humiliated that you didn't manage to stop the bullies insulting you or stop them saying untrue or unfair things. Remember that you did as well as you could in a tricky situation. It's usually only in films that the hero gets the bullies to eat their words too.

If you have been beaten up, you'll also need to talk about it with an adult you trust. You'll need to discuss whether you want to make a complaint against the people who hurt you and how to make sure this situation doesn't happen again. You may need to see a doctor. Above all, you'll need time to get your confidence back. Remember, you didn't deserve to be beaten up and it's OK to feel angry about it. It's OK to feel upset about it too.

Your confidence and self-esteem will also need rebuilding. If you are feeling sad and down you may find it useful to talk to a counsellor. If your school doesn't have a school counsellor, your parents could ask your doctor to recommend one.

STOPPING BEING A BULLY: SENSIBLE STRATEGIES

If you are a bully, it's possible to spend the rest of your life in win/lose situations. That is you 'win' when you bully someone and they lose. But do you really win? You are not going to be offered real friendship and respect by people you bully or by people who see you bully. They can only fear you. You don't need to lead your life in this sad way; you can change your behaviour.

Perhaps underneath your tough exterior, you don't always feel confident and you'd like to find ways of feeling more secure inside. Here are some ideas that may be helpful:

- Observe how relaxed, confident, happy people get on together without needing to bully or control each other. Are there ways of doing things here that you can learn from?
- Are you a bully because you are bullied at home – by your parents or by older brothers or sisters? If this is so, you know how painful it is to be bullied. Think of how you would like to be treated and start trying to treat yourself and other people in these good ways.
- Do you find it humiliating when you get something wrong or make a mistake? Perhaps you try to make yourself feel better by putting someone else 'in the wrong' and giving them a

hard time. But we all make mistakes and get things wrong from time to time – it's a natural part of learning how to do things. Perhaps you could try being kinder to yourself.

- Why not put your physical energies and aggression into sport? It's OK to win there by beating other people so long as you stick to the rules of the game. Watch the athletes you admire on television and find out if you could train for that sport.

- Think about the pain that verbal bullying can cause – as much as, if not more than, physical bullying. (Sometimes people just don't realise how much words can hurt and that they are being bullies when they talk to or jeer at people.)

- Why not be a leader, but without trying to dominate and control other people? Good leaders are people who look after their team or group, making sure everyone is treated fairly and everyone's point of view is heard. Perhaps joining an Outward Bound course, like Guides or Scouts, is something that might channel and develop your leadership skills.

- Think about the heroes you admire in films, books or television. Are they people who settle arguments by punching, shooting and knifing 'enemies' like so many film and TV characters? If so, try to think of other heroes – for example, such real-life people

126

as Mahatma Gandhi or Nelson Mandela, who won through by using other kinds of strength.

- What is it about the people that you bully that irritates you? You might not realise, say, that Peter always looks timid because you frighten him; Yvonne is clumsy because she was born with a defect of the hips that cannot be cured; Jane would love to have nice clothes like the other girls in class, but her family cannot afford them. And so forth. Try to see other people as whole people and as different from you as you are different from them.

- Do you enjoy bullying because you enjoy showing off in front of an audience? It's possible to get that kind of enjoyment without hurting other people – for example by acting in a school play or being good at sports. Why not try these instead?

- Do you feel anxious and insecure about your sexual or gender identity? Do you worry about whether you come over as 'properly' masculine or 'properly' feminine? Or that you might be gay? Taunting others with sexual or homophobic abuse may be your way to try to appear confident at others' expense. But just being the kind of young man or young woman you are becoming is absolutely fine. Remember, everyone is individual, unique and different.

- Do you find it difficult when other people have different opinions from you about things or different ways of doing things? Perhaps it feels threatening or it makes you anxious. You wish everyone were the same. But it's OK for other people to think or do things the way it suits them and for you to think and do things the way it suits you. There is room for difference.
- Do you find that tension builds up inside you and that you are spoiling for a fight in order to release it? Could you find ways to talk about it instead? A school counsellor may be able to help you talk about your feelings.

WHAT TO DO IF YOU WITNESS BULLYING

If you witness bullying behaviour you could try:

- to be a friend to the person who is being bullied. You can let them know that you have seen how they are treated and you think it is wrong. You may fear that doing this would result in you being bullied as well, but even your background support would probably be welcome;
- helping the person who is bullied to tell an adult about what is happening. Perhaps you could offer to go with them;
- telling the person who is bullied about the

helplines listed at the end of this book;
- encouraging the discussion of anti-bullying issues in school and/or bringing them up at the school council if there is one;
- talking to your friends if they are the bullies. Try to help them to see that their behaviour is damaging and, if you dare, that you disapprove of it;
- asking your school counsellor (if there is one) for advice.

Conclusion

Bullying has long been an event that children have had to suffer alone. Now at last bullying is being openly discussed and, if you are being bullied, there are ways that you can help yourself and ways that you can find help. You don't have to suffer alone. At the end of this book, I suggest people and organisations you can contact if you are going through a hard time. Realising that you deserve to be well treated is an important step and I hope that this book has helped you to believe this is true.

If you are a bully, it is also possible to help yourself and to get help so that you no longer need to hurt others in this unhappy and destructive fashion. You too deserve to feel better about yourself and I hope that this book has helped you to réalise that this is possible.

Most people believe strongly in fairness and want to

treat others with care and respect and be well treated in return. Bullying is immensely disturbing, even if you yourself are not the one who is bullied. I hope this book has helped you to see ways in which you might contribute to the creation of a world where people can feel more confident and at ease.

Questions and Answers

Q.

Isn't bullying just normal? It's always happened and it always will. Shouldn't people just toughen up and deal with it themselves?

A.

Unfortunately bullying is something that happens all too often so, yes, children should learn to deal with it, hopefully with help from sympathetic adults. On the other hand, it is not 'normal' for people – adults or children – to live in an atmosphere of fear and insecurity, which is what happens when bullying is allowed to go on.

Some people do manage to deal with bullying on their own without being too hurt by it – generally they are people with high self-esteem (lots of 'inner power') who do not allow bullying to influence how they see themselves. Other people, whose self-esteem is more fragile, find bullying very distressing and they lose confidence in themselves. Sometimes bullying can be so long term or so vicious that even the most confident person would find it impossible to deal with on their own.

People who have been bullied can suffer from the effects even in later life, finding it hard to trust other people, hard to form relationships and hard to have any confidence in their own worth. Children who are bullied may become truants, fall behind with their work, suffer from depression and have even, in some cases, committed suicide.

All this amounts to very good reasons for children who are bullied to seek adult help as soon as possible rather than try to deal with it purely on their own.

Q.
You say that if you are bullied or teased you should try not to let the bullies see how upset you are. Isn't it harmful to bottle up your feelings like this? And why shouldn't the bullies and teasers know how hurt you are feeling?

A.
Part of growing up is learning when it is appropriate to show your feelings and when it's not. It's not a good idea to show the people who are tormenting you that they are succeeding in upsetting and hurting you, if

you can avoid it. Sometimes of course, it's just not possible not to cry or not to look as frightened as you feel. But if you are able to appear indifferent, this may reduce or stop the teasing or bullying. Those people who bully and tease do so to get a reaction from their victim – they want to know that they have succeeded in hurting or upsetting or embarrassing you. If you don't react, they may stop doing it.

Of course you need to talk about what happened when you were bullied or teased and how painful and hurtful it was, but you should do this with people you trust and know are on your side. After such a horrible experience you need to be with people with whom you feel secure.

Q.

Do child bullies grow up to be adult bullies?

A.

If child bullies are not helped to find other ways of dealing with their aggression or other troubling feelings, it is very possible (although not inevitable) that they will continue to bully and be aggressive in adult life. This is a sad way to live a life.

People sometimes find the idea that bullies deserve understanding hard to take when bullies do such horrible and mean things to others. But it is very important that children who bully get sympathetic adult help so that they can be released from the pain and fear that they express in their bullying behaviour and learn happier ways to get on with other people. Also, someone who is being a bully might be doing it because they too are being bullied.

Q.

I am really embarrassed about my middle name and I haven't told anyone what it is. My friend saw it written in the school register and now she's threatening to tell everyone. I'll die if she tells.

A.

Nobody died from having a middle name they hated. Why not take the wind out of your so-called friend's sails by telling everyone about it yourself? You could say something like: 'I don't know what my parents could have been thinking of.' Don't let people like your 'friend' torment you in this way – few personal things are really as embarrassing as they seem.

Q.

My ears stick out and I get called 'jug-ears' at school. I tried growing my hair to hide them, but people still make fun of me.

A.

You're in good company – the future King of England's ears stick out too. Remember that teasers will go on making fun so long as you let them see that you are reacting. Try to imagine that your head is enclosed in a giant bubble. When you are teased the teasing can't break through the bubble – it just bounces off.

IMAGINE THAT YOUR HEAD IS ENCLOSED
IN A GIANT BUBBLE

Q.

Isn't advising people to list all the things they are good at and the nice things people have said about them just going to encourage them to be big-headed?

A.

If that were true, more children should be big-headed, if that means that they are aware of the things they have done well and feel pleased with themselves. In fact, a lot of parents and teachers don't give as much praise and encouragement as children need and deserve. If you listen to the way parents and teachers talk to children, you'll find that most of the time they are telling them what not to do, not praising them for things they have done well.

Q.

I got beaten up walking home from school by some white kids, the same ones who call me bad names in school. There aren't many black kids in my school, so there's no one to help.

A.

As I explain in this book, racist bullying is something that schools are now much more aware of. If your school is not supporting you as it should, can you seek help from your family or a trusted member of your community? If you have been attacked, you may want to consider reporting what happened to the police. Racist attacks are against the law.

If you have trouble getting support, do contact one of the agencies listed at the end of this book. It may take some time to get your confidence back after such a horrible event. Once you do, it might be helpful to find out more about the history and contribution to society of black people in the UK, as you may discover role models whose achievements will encourage and inspire you and help you to feel less alone.

Q.

I told my friend that I might be gay and she promised not to tell anyone, but now she has. I dread going to school, as people are saying terrible things to me. The teachers do nothing to stop them.

A.

It is a very hard thing that, just at a point in your life when it's often difficult feeling you are different from everyone else, you are having to sort out what it might mean to be gay. Try to remember that being gay is not in itself a problem – it's the fear, ignorance and prejudice that some people have about homosexuality that is the problem.

Homophobic (anti-gay) bullying is an issue that your school should take seriously. If this is not happening, are you able to get support from your parents or some other trustworthy adult? If you feel completely alone, do get in touch with one of the support agencies listed at the end of this book. If you feel despairing, ring a helpline and talk in confidence about what is happening. There are people who know just how it is to be a young, isolated gay person. You may think you are the only gay person in your school, but there is a good chance other people there – students or teachers – are lesbian or gay too. It might be that they are not as brave as you are or even that they haven't realised what their feelings mean yet.

Where to Get Help and Advice

When you need help, try to talk to someone you trust – perhaps your parents or your teacher. If you don't have anyone you can talk to, contact these organisations. You can ring and chat without even giving your name, if you want to. Many of them are in London, but some have branches in different parts of the country that they can put you in touch with.

Phone numbers starting 080 are free to call from a BT landline and won't show up on the phone bill. However, these calls aren't free from most mobiles and may appear on the bill. Numbers starting 0845 are charged at local (cheap) rates on BT landlines and mobiles wherever in the country you call from, but they'll be on the phone bill.

HELPLINES

Some of these help and advice lines are free (you don't need a card or money, just dial the number) and are open 24 hours.

ChildLine

www.childline.org.uk

Helpline: 0800 1111 (open 24 hours)

Provides excellent (and confidential) advice and help for children and young people in trouble or in danger. Very experienced at dealing with bullying. Because of high demand, it can be difficult to get through, but do keep trying.

Samaritans

www.samaritans.org

National helpline: 08457 90 90 90 (UK and Northern Ireland)

1850 60 90 90 (Republic of Ireland)

24-hour helpline for people with any problems.

London Lesbian and Gay Switchboard

www.llgs.org.uk

Helpline: 0300 330 0630

24-hour counselling for lesbian and gay people. Because of high demand, it can be difficult to get through, but do keep trying.

WEBSITES

Pupiline

www.pupiline.net

This website was set up by a bullied teenager and is a place for victims of bullying to chat and help and support each other, and lists other helpful websites.

BBC Schools: Student Life

www.bbc.co.uk/schools/studentlife/schoolissues/bullying/beat_the_bullies.shtml

Information and advice for young people.

SafeKids.Com

www.safekids.com

Useful advice on countering cyber-bullying and keeping safe online. Includes SafeTeens.com.

Stonewall

www.stonewall.org.uk

Excellent information on what to do about homophobic (anti-gay) bullying. A teacher's pack and a pupil's pack are available.

It Gets Better

www.youtube.com (search for It Gets Better)

It Gets Better is an internet-based project started in the US following the suicide of a number of teenagers who were bullied because they were gay, or thought to be gay. Adult gay people including many celebrities talk on YouTube and aim to reassure young gay people that 'it will get better'. Other well-known people such as Barack Obama have also taken part.

STOP Cyberbullying
www.stopcyberbullying.org
An online campaign with useful information and advice.

The Metropolitan Police
www.safe.met.police.uk/bullying/get_the_facts.html
Information on bullying, cyber-bullying, internet safety and the law.

ORGANISATIONS

Advisory Centre for Education (ACE)
www.ace-ed.org.uk
Advice line: 0808 800 5793 (freephone)
Advice for parents, teachers and governors on state education in England and Wales and on anti-bullying policies in schools.

Anti–Bullying Network
www.antibullying.net
Aims to support anti-bullying work in schools.

Bullying Online

www.bullying.co.uk

Parentline: 0808 800 2222

Help for teachers and parents of bullied children. It also offers an advice page for young victims.

Changing Faces

www.changingfaces.org.uk

Tel: 0845 4500 275

Help and advice for people with facial disfigurements and disfiguring conditions.

The Children's Legal Centre

www.childrenslegalcentre.com

Tel: 0808 802 0008

Legal advice on every area to do with children's rights, including bullying.

The Department for Education and Skills

www.education.gov.uk/schools/pupilsupport/behaviour/bullying

Useful information for parents and teachers on responding to bullying and anti-bullying policies.

Equality and Human Rights Commission

www.equalityhumanrights.com

Tel: 0845 604 6610 (England)

Tel: 0845 604 5510 (Scotland)

Tel: 0845 604 8810 (Wales)

Advice on racial discrimination or attacks.

Family and Friends of Lesbians and Gays (FFLAG)

www.fflag.org.uk

Tel: 0845 652 0311

Advice and support for parents.

The Intercom Trust

www.intercomtrust.org.uk

Tel: 0800 612 3010

Information on Action Against Homophobic Bullying which supports and informs anti-bullying policies in schools.

Kidscape

www.kidscape.org.uk

Helpline: 08451 205 204 (local rates)

A charity dedicated to preventing bullying and child sexual abuse. Their helpline is for parents, guardians, relatives and friends of bullied children. For children who are experiencing bullying, they recommend contacting ChildLine.

Lesbian and Gay Christian Movement (LGCM)

www.lgcm.org.uk

Counselling helpline: 020 7739 1249

Advice and support for young gay people.

Young Minds

www.youngminds.org.uk

Promotes the mental health of children, young people and their families. Advice and information on bullying.

In Ireland

The Anti-Bullying Centre

www.abc.tcd.ie

Counselling and advice service for school, parents and organisations.

FURTHER READING

There are lots of novels with bullying as a theme to look out for – such as Michael Coleman's *Weirdo's War*, Keith Gray's *Malarkey*, Judy Blume's *Blubber*, Elizabeth Laird's *Secret Friends* and Anne Fine's *The Tulip Touch*.

You can find more information about other such books on the Books for Keeps website: www.booksforkeeps.co.uk.

Index